GRAPHIC ORGANIZERS
AND OTHER
VISUAL STRATEGIES

ENGAGE THE
BRAIN

MARCIA L. TATE

CORWIN PRESS
Classroom

For information:

Corwin Press
A SAGE Publications Company
2455 Teller Road
Thousand Oaks, California 91320
CorwinPress.com

SAGE Publications, Ltd.
1 Oliver's Yard
55 City Road
London EC1Y 1SP
United Kingdom

SAGE Publications India Pvt. Ltd.
B 1/I 1 Mohan Cooperative
Industrial Area
Mathura Road, New Delhi
India 110 044

SAGE Publications Asia-Pacific Pvt. Ltd.
33 Pekin Street #02-01
Far East Square
Singapore 048763

Printed in the United States of America.

ISBN 978-1-4129-5228-6

This book is printed on acid-free paper.

08 09 10 11 12 10 9 8 7 6 5 4 3 2 1

Executive Editor: Kathleen Hex
Managing Developmental Editor: Christine Hood
Editorial Assistant: Anne O'Dell
Developmental Writer: Jeanine Manfro
Developmental Editor: Carolea Williams
Proofreader: Bette Darwin
Art Director: Anthony D. Paular
Cover Designer: Monique Hahn
Interior Production Artist: Scott Van Atta
Illustrator: Corbin Hillam
Design Consultant: PUMPKiN PIE Design

GRADE **4**

TABLE OF CONTENTS

Connections to Standards

This chart shows the national academic standards that are covered in each chapter.

MATHEMATICS	Standards are covered on pages
Numbers and Operations 1	9, 13, 20, 24, 26
Numbers and Operations 2	9, 13, 20
Numbers and Operations 3	9, 20
Algebra 1	20
Algebra 2	9, 13, 20
Algebra 3	9, 13, 24
Geometry 1	17
Geometry 2	20
Communication 2	24
Communication 4	24
Representation 1	26

SCIENCE	Standards are covered on pages
Science as Inquiry 1, 2	32
Physical Science 1, 2, 3	48
Life Science 1, 2	28
Life Science 3	28, 45
Earth and Space Science 1	37, 40, 42
Earth and Space Science 2	42
Earth and Space Science 3	37, 40, 42, 45
Science in Personal and Social Perspectives 4	42, 45

SOCIAL STUDIES	Standards are covered on pages
Social Studies 1	53, 56, 59, 64
Social Studies 2	53, 56, 59, 62, 64
Social Studies 3	50, 53, 56, 59, 67
Social Studies 4	56, 64
Social Studies 5	50, 53, 56
Social Studies 6	50, 56
Social Studies 7	56
Social Studies 8	62
Social Studies 9	50
Social Studies 10	50

LANGUAGE ARTS	Standards are covered on pages
Language Arts 1	59, 64, 67, 70, 73, 76, 82, 87
Language Arts 2	64, 73, 76
Language Arts 3	59, 64, 67, 70, 73, 76, 82
Language Arts 4	59, 64, 73, 76, 79, 82, 85
Language Arts 5	59, 73, 76, 79, 82, 87
Language Arts 6	59, 64, 70, 73, 76, 79, 82, 85
Language Arts 7	79, 82
Language Arts 8	64, 70, 82, 85
Language Arts 11	73, 76, 79, 82
Language Arts 12	73, 76, 79, 82, 85

Introduction

An ancient Chinese proverb claims: "Tell me, I forget. Show me, I remember. Involve me, I understand." This timeless saying insinuates what all educators should know: Unless students are involved and actively engaged in learning, true learning rarely occurs.

The latest brain research reveals that both the right and left hemispheres of the brain should be engaged in the learning process. This is important because the hemispheres talk to one another over the corpus callosum, the structure that connects them. No strategies are better designed for this purpose than graphic organizers and visuals. Both of these strategies engage students' visual modality. More information goes into the brain visually than through any other modality. Therefore, it makes sense to take advantage of students' visual strengths to reinforce and make sense of learning.

How to Use This Book

The activities in this book cover the content areas and are designed using strategies that actively engage the brain. They are presented in the way the brain learns best, to make sure students get the most out of each lesson: focus activity, modeling, guided practice, check for understanding, independent practice, and closing. Go through each step to ensure that students will be fully engaged in the concept being taught and understand its purpose and meaning.

Each step-by-step activity provides one or more visual tools students can use to make important connections between related concepts, structure their thinking, organize ideas logically, and reinforce learning. Graphic organizers and visuals include: factor trees, sequence chart, word web, Venn diagram, posters, artifacts, T-chart, thematic map, picture glossary, cluster map, bulletin board display, fishbone map, color wheel, spider map, and more!

These brain-compatible activities are sure to engage and motivate every student's brain in your classroom! Watch your students change from passive to active learners as they process visual concepts into learning that is not only fun, but also remembered for a lifetime.

Put It Into Practice

Lecture and repetitive worksheets have long been the traditional way of delivering knowledge and reinforcing learning. While some higher-achieving students may engage in this type of learning, educators now know that actively engaging students' brains is not a luxury, but a necessity if students are truly to acquire and retain content, not only for tests, but for life.

The 1990s were dubbed the Decade of the Brain, because millions of dollars were spent on brain research. Educators today should know more about how students learn than ever before. Learning style theories that call for student engagement have been proposed for decades, as evidenced by research such as Howard Gardner's theory of multiple intelligences (1983), Bernice McCarthy's 4MAT Model (1990), and VAKT (visual, auditory, kinesthetic, tactile) learning styles theories.

I have identified 20 strategies that, according to brain research and learning style theory, appear to correlate with the way the brain learns best. I have observed hundreds of teachers—regular education, special education, and gifted. Regardless of the classification or grade level of the students, exemplary teachers consistently use these 20 strategies to deliver memorable classroom instruction and help their students understand and retain vast amounts of content.

These 20 brain-based instructional strategies include the following:

1. Brainstorming and Discussion

2. Drawing and Artwork

3. Field Trips

4. Games

5. Graphic Organizers, Semantic Maps, and Word Webs

6. Humor

7. Manipulatives, Experiments, Labs, and Models

8. Metaphors, Analogies, and Similes

9. Mnemonic Devices

10. Movement

11. Music, Rhythm, Rhyme, and Rap

12. Project-based and Problem-based Instruction

13. Reciprocal Teaching and Cooperative Learning

14. Role Plays, Drama, Pantomimes, Charades

15. Storytelling

16. Technology

17. Visualization and Guided Imagery

18. Visuals

19. Work Study and Apprenticeships

20. Writing and Journals

This book features Strategy 5: Graphic Organizers, Semantic Maps, and Word Webs, and Strategy 18: Visuals. Both of these strategies focus on integrating the visual and verbal elements of learning. Picture thinking, visual thinking, and visual/spatial learning is the phenomenon of thinking through visual processing. Since 90% of the brain's sensory input comes from visual sources, it stands to reason that the most powerful influence on learners' behavior is concrete, visual images. (Jensen, 1994) In addition, linking verbal and visual images increases students' ability to store and retrieve information. (Ogle, 2000)

Graphic organizers are visual representations of linear ideas that benefit both left and right hemispheres of the brain. They assist us in making sense of information, enable us to search for patterns, and provide an organized tool for making important conceptual connections. Graphic organizers, also known as word webs or semantic, mind, and concept maps, can be used to plan lessons or present information to students. Once familiar with the technique, students should be able to construct their own graphic organizers, reflecting their understanding of the concepts taught.

Because we live in a highly visual world, using visuals as a teaching strategy makes sense. Each day, students are overwhelmed with images from video games, computers, and television. Visual strategies capitalize specifically on the one modality that many students use consistently and have developed extensively—the visual modality. Types of visuals include overheads, maps, graphs, charts, and other concrete objects and artifacts that clarify learning. Since so much sensory input comes from visual sources, pictures, words, and learning-related artifacts around the classroom take on exaggerated importance in students' brains. Visuals such as these provide learning support and constant reinforcement.

These memorable strategies help students make sense of learning by focusing on the ways the brain learns best. Fully supported by the latest brain research, these strategies provide the tools you need to boost motivation, energy, and most important, the academic achievement of your students.

CHAPTER 1

Mathematics

Through the Forest: Factor Trees

Skills Objectives

Use multiplication to show the factors of a number.

Identify prime numbers.

Draw a factor tree for a given number.

Materials

Multiplication Chart reproducible

Through the Forest reproducible

A **Factor Tree** is a graphic organizer that shows how a number can be broken down into a unique set of prime factors. Using factor trees helps students see that many products of multiplication can be reached in a number of ways. Students also learn that no matter which numbers are multiplied to reach a given product, the prime factors will be the same.

1. Focus students' attention on factors by displaying a multiplication chart. Have students identify all of the places on the chart that show the number *12*. List the corresponding multiplication problems on the board. (*1 x 12, 2 x 6, 3 x 4, 4 x 3, 6 x 2,* and *12 x 1*)

2. Tell students that the numbers *1, 2, 3, 4, 6,* and *12* are all *factors* of the number *12*. Explain that factors are numbers that divide evenly into a given number.

3. Tell students that some numbers do not have any factors other than 1 and themselves. These numbers are called *prime numbers*. Using the multiplication chart, point out how the numbers *2, 3, 5, 7,* and *11* are all prime numbers.

4. Explain that a factor tree shows all the factors used to reach a number. The object of a factor tree is to show the prime numbers that are multiplied to reach the given number.

5. Model how to draw a factor tree on the board. Guide students to draw one with you.

6. Give students a copy of the **Multiplication Chart** and **Through the Forest reproducibles (pages 11–12)**. Instruct them to identify numbers on the multiplication chart that have at least four factors. Have students write one such number in the top box of each tree on the Through the Forest reproducible.

7. For independent practice, instruct students to create factor trees for the numbers they selected. Before they begin, make sure they understand how to complete the trees all the way down to the prime numbers.

8. Once students complete their factor trees, invite volunteers to share their work with the class. Ask them to draw one sample factor tree on the board. Help them correct any mistakes on their trees. Ask students to raise their hands if they drew the same tree on their papers. Have those students give a thumbs-up or thumbs-down to indicate if their trees show the same prime numbers as the one on the board.

Extended Learning

- Have students make flashcards that show the factors of different numbers.
- Have students work on fact families for multiplication and division. Give them a set of three numbers, such as 5, 7, and 35 and have them write the two multiplication problems and two division problems that use those numbers.
- Have students look for patterns in the multiplication chart. For example, all multiples of 10 end in 0.

Multiplication Chart

x	1	2	3	4	5	6	7	8	9	10	11	12
1	1	2	3	4	5	6	7	8	9	10	11	12
2	2	4	6	8	10	12	14	16	18	20	22	24
3	3	6	9	12	15	18	21	24	27	30	33	36
4	4	8	12	16	20	24	28	32	36	40	44	48
5	5	10	15	20	25	30	35	40	45	50	55	60
6	6	12	18	24	30	36	42	48	54	60	66	72
7	7	14	21	28	35	42	49	56	63	70	77	84
8	8	16	24	32	40	48	56	64	72	80	88	96
9	9	18	27	36	45	54	63	72	81	90	99	108
10	10	20	30	40	50	60	70	80	90	100	110	120
11	11	22	33	44	55	66	77	88	99	110	121	132
12	12	24	36	48	60	72	84	96	108	120	132	144

Through the Forest

Directions: Look for numbers on your multiplication chart that have at least four factors. Choose one of these numbers for each tree. Write the number in the box at the top of the tree. Draw a factor tree for the number. Be sure that each number at the bottom of the factor tree is a prime number.

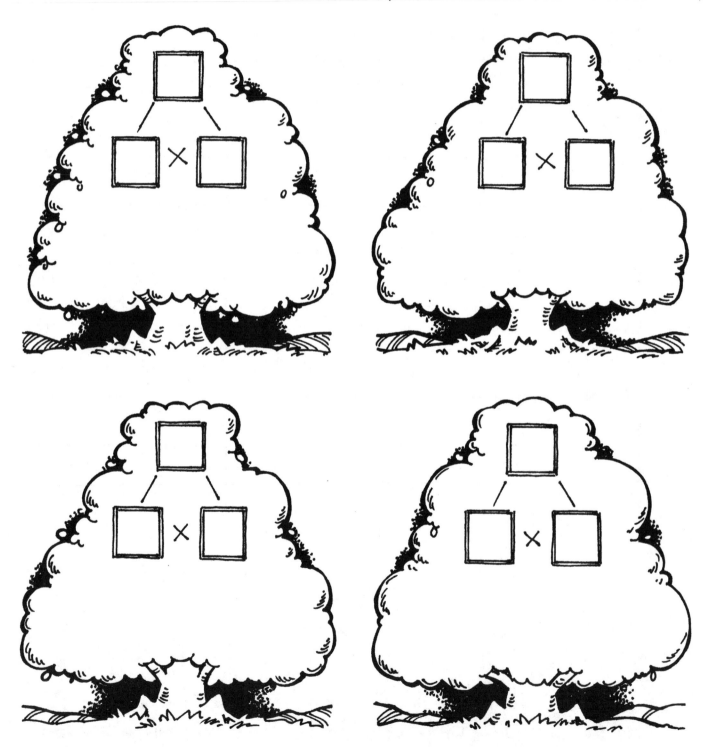

Order in the Court: Sequence Chart/ Word Web

Skills Objectives

Understand and use the proper order of operations when solving multiple-step equations.

Use parentheses to indicate which operation to perform first.

Create a mnemonic to help remember the order of operations.

Materials

Order in the Court reproducible

Mighty Mnemonics reproducible

A **Sequence Chart** is a graphic organizer used to represent a sequence of events or procedures. In this activity, students complete a sequence chart to demonstrate their understanding of the order of operations. They then use a **Word Web** to create a mnemonic for remembering the order of operations.

1. To focus attention on the need for an order of operations, write this problem on the board: *3 + 12 ÷ 3 − 2 + 6 x 3*. Ask several volunteers to come to the board and work out solutions to the problem. Have them explain the order in which they solved the problem.

2. Tell students that there can be only one right answer to the equation. Explain that there is a specific order in which the different operations are to be solved to arrive at the correct answer. This is called the *order of operations*.

3. Explain that there are three steps in the order of operations. (Note: The step for exponents has been eliminated since it is covered in later grades.) List the steps on the board.

Step 1: Solve any problems inside of parentheses.

Step 2: Solve all multiplication and division problems in order from left to right.

Step 3: Solve all addition and subtraction problems in order from left to right.

4. Use the sample problem to model using the order of operations.

$$3 + \underline{12 \div 3} - 2 + 6 \times 3$$
$$3 + 4 - 2 + \underline{6 \times 3}$$
$$\underline{3 + 4} - 2 + 18$$
$$\underline{7 - 2} + 18$$
$$\underline{5 + 18}$$
$$23$$

5. For guided practice, present several more sample problems on the board. Include some problems with parentheses and some without. Invite volunteers to solve the problems, showing each step of the solution separately. Encourage students to use parentheses in problems that don't already have them to help keep track of which operation to perform first.

6. Give students a copy of the **Order in the Court reproducible (page 15)**. Instruct them to complete the sequence chart to show the order of operations. Check to make sure they remember the steps before they begin.

7. When students have completed the sequence chart, ask them to create a silly sentence to help them remember the steps in the order of operations. Explain that this memory technique is called a *mnemonic device*. Write the letters *P, M, D, A, S* on the board. Explain that the letters represent the words used in the order of operations—**P**arenthesis, **M**ultiplication and **D**ivision, **A**ddition and **S**ubtraction. Point out that these five words represent three steps.

8. Have students brainstorm words that begin with each letter and write them on the board. Use circles and lines to connect the words and letters in a web. Ask volunteers to use the words in sentences, such as *Pizza Makes Donkeys Act Silly* or *Polly's Mom Drives A Suburban*.

9. After brainstorming a few silly sentences together, give students a copy of the **Mighty Mnemonics reproducible (page 16)**. Invite them to brainstorm words for each letter, and create unique sentences to help them remember the order of operations. For closure, have students read their sentences aloud for the class.

Extended Learning

- Invite students to make posters illustrating their mnemonic sentences. Display posters around the room as additional visual aids for the concept.

- Have students write multistep problems for each other to solve.

Name _____ Date _____

Mighty Mnemonics

Directions: Write a silly sentence to help you remember the order of operations. Brainstorm words that begin with each letter. Use the words to write your sentence.

pizza | pretty
P
presents | Paul
puppies

donuts
dig | dolphins
D
deliver | dive
slowly | sun
S
slide | spaghetti
sandwiches

make | Mom
M
move | money
munch

apple
always | avocado
A
afternoon | and

Write your sentence here:
Puppies munch donuts and spaghetti

Order in the Court

Directions: Write the steps for the order of operations on the gavels. First, write the words from the Word Box on the handles. Then write the rule for each operation on the head of the gavel.

Word Box		
Multiplication and Division	Addition and Subtraction	Parenthesis

Mighty Mnemonics

Directions: Write a silly sentence to help you remember the order of operations. Brainstorm words that begin with each letter. Use the words to write your sentence.

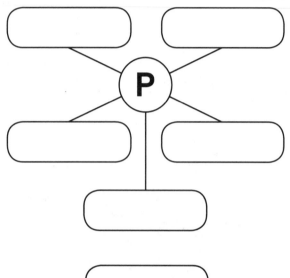

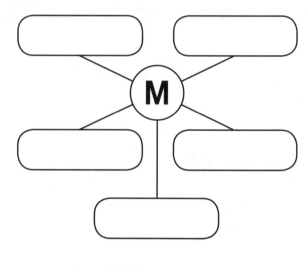

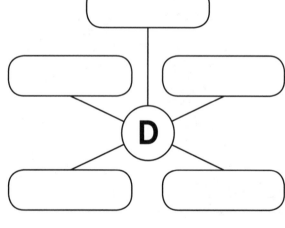

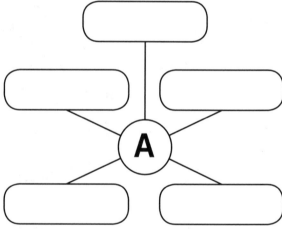

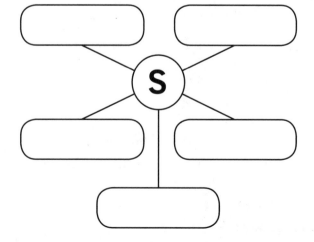

Write your sentence here:

_____

_____

_____

Shape Up: Chart Matrix

Skills Objectives
Analyze characteristics and properties of geometric solids.
Compare and contrast characteristics and properties of various solids.

Materials
Shape Machine reproducible

solid geometric shapes (rectangular prisms, triangular prisms, cylinders, cubes, square pyramids, cones)

A **Chart Matrix** helps students organize information about several traits related to the same topic. In this activity, students use a chart matrix to describe geometric solids. They record the names of three-dimensional shapes as well as the number of faces, edges, and vertices for each one. Students can then use the matrix to compare and contrast different features of the shapes.

1. Display and have students name the geometric shapes that they will be working with. Then review the following definitions.

   > **face:** the flat side of a solid figure
   > **edge:** the line segment or line that is an intersection of two faces
   > **vertex:** a point common to the edges of a solid figure, the corners

2. Divide students into small groups. Give each group a set of solid geometric shapes. Invite students to explore the shapes for a few moments. Then give each student a copy of the **Shape Machine reproducible (page 19)**.

3. Model how to complete the chart matrix. Guide students to enter information on the matrix for the rectangular prism. Have students write the name of the shape on the chart, draw a picture, and record the numbers of faces (*6*), edges (*12*), and vertices (*8*).

4. Check to make sure students understand how to complete the matrix before directing them to work in their groups. Invite groups to analyze each shape and complete the chart.

5. When students have completed their charts, close the activity by having them make comparisons between the shapes. Ask questions such as, *Which shape has the fewest number of vertices? Which shapes have the most faces? Can you explain the differences between these two shapes?*

Extended Learning

- Have students expand the charts by examining more complicated shapes such as an octahedron, a dodecahedron, and an icosahedron.
- Invite students to build paper models of geometric solids. Many patterns for building the models can be found at Enchanted Learning: *www.enchantedlearning.com.*
- Have students complete a Venn diagram to compare and contrast two different shapes.

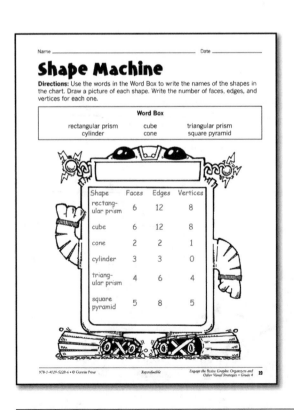

Shape Machine

Directions: Use the words in the Word Box to write the names of the shapes in the chart. Draw a picture of each shape. Write the number of faces, edges, and vertices for each one.

Word Box		
rectangular prism	cube	triangular prism
cylinder	cone	square pyramid

Follow the Rule: T-Chart

Materials

Follow the Rule reproducible

Coordinate Grid reproducible

overhead projector

Battleship board game (Milton Bradley)

Skills Objectives

Use letters to stand for numbers in simple equations.
Use coordinate grids to represent points and graph lines.

In math, a **T-Chart** can be used to list and record the answers to simple algebraic equations. In this activity, students read an algebraic expression, determine the rule for the expression, and use a T-chart to list possible outcomes for following the rule. Students will then plot the answers for each rule on a coordinate grid.

1. Introduce the concept of coordinate grids by giving students the opportunity to play the game Battleship. While they are playing, use a sheet of graph paper to make a coordinate grid with and x-axis and a y-axis. Copy the graph paper onto an overhead transparency.

2. Explain to students that while they were playing Battleship, they were working with a coordinate grid system. Use the transparency to review coordinate grids with students. Point out that the horizontal line is the x-axis and the vertical line is the y-axis. Demonstrate plotting several points on the grid. Name different points and call on volunteers to plot them.

3. Write a simple algebraic expression on a blank transparency, such as 3x = y. Draw a T-chart below the expression and model how to use the chart to record different values for x and y.

4. Explain that the rule for the equation is to multiply the numbers in the x column by 3 to get the numbers in the y column.

3x	=	y
x		y
2		6
4		12
6		18

5. Guide students as they practice the concept with other rules. Include the use of negative numbers.

6. Tell students that the numbers in the T-chart will become ordered pairs for a coordinate grid. Have them help you plot the ordered pairs on the grid transparency.

7. Give students a copy of the **Follow the Rule** and **Coordinate Grid reproducibles (pages 22–23)**. Check to make sure students understand how to work with the expressions to compile lists of ordered pairs. Encourage them to use different colored pencils for each rule on the Follow the Rule reproducible. Then, as they plot the ordered pairs on the Coordinate Grid, they can use the same color of pencil for each set.

8. To close the lesson, have volunteers use the overhead transparencies to share their work with the class.

Extended Learning

- Have students draw simple shapes on a grid and then list the ordered pairs used to make the shapes. Invite student pairs to plot each other's shapes.
- Have students work in pairs to write simple algebraic expressions and use T-charts to list possible outcomes.

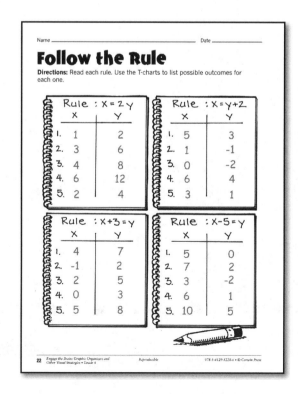

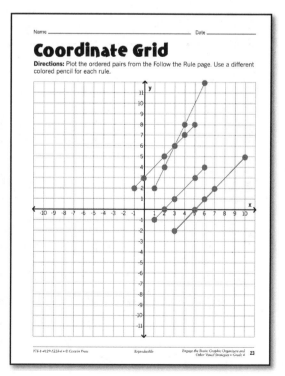

Name ______________________________ Date ______________

Follow the Rule

Directions: Read each rule. Use the T-charts to list possible outcomes for each one.

Rule : $X = 2Y$

	X	Y
1.		
2.		
3.		
4.		
5.		

Rule : $X = Y + 2$

	X	Y
1.		
2.		
3.		
4.		
5.		

Rule : $X + 3 = Y$

	X	Y
1.		
2.		
3.		
4.		
5.		

Rule : $X - 5 = Y$

	X	Y
1.		
2.		
3.		
4.		
5.		

978-1-4129-5228-6

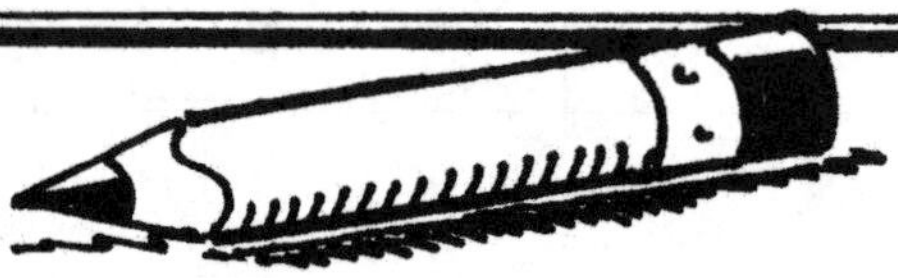

Coordinate Grid

Directions: Plot the ordered pairs from the Follow the Rule page. Use a different colored pencil for each rule.

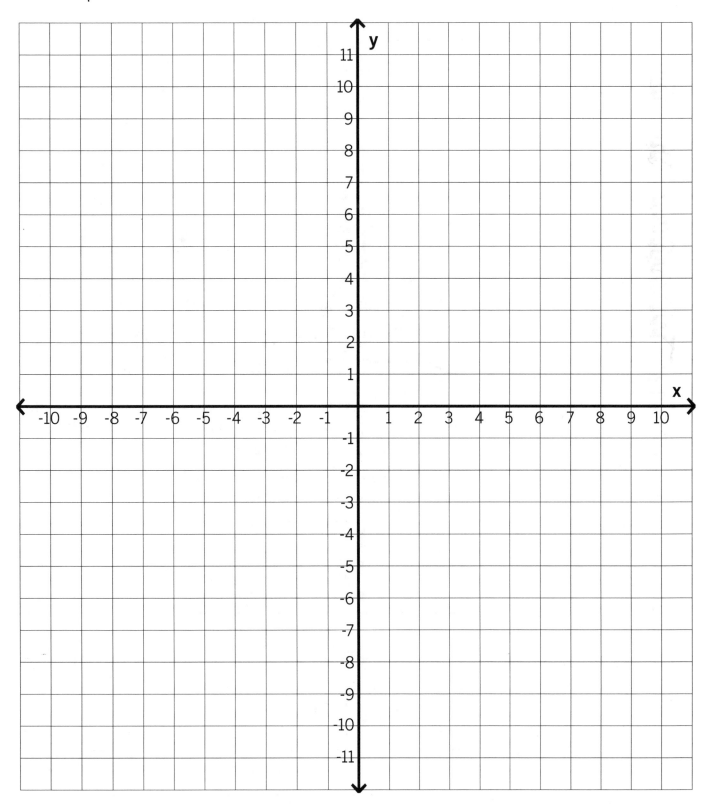

Fruit Fractions: Real Artifacts

Skills Objectives

Demonstrate knowledge of fractions.

Work with equivalent fractions.

Compare improper fractions to mixed numbers.

Using **Real Artifacts** is a valuable visual strategy to clarify a concept. In this exercise, students have the opportunity for hands-on learning as they work with fractions. Students work in groups to cut real pieces of fruit into fractional segments. This activity helps them learn to order fractions from smallest to greatest and to understand equivalency.

1. Introduce this activity by giving several students one orange each. Ask them how they might go about dividing the orange so that different groups of students would all get an equal share.

2. Draw a large rectangle on the board, and divide it into six equal sections. Divide the first section in half, the second section into

$\frac{1}{2}$							
$\frac{1}{3}$							
$\frac{1}{4}$							
$\frac{1}{5}$							
$\frac{1}{6}$							
$\frac{1}{8}$							

thirds, the third section into fourths, the fourth section into fifths, the fifth section into sixths, and the last section into eighths.

3. Review with students the parts of a fraction. Explain that the *denominator* tells the total number of parts in a set and the *numerator* tells the number of parts taken from the denominator. Refer to the chart you drew on the board and have students answer questions such as: *Which section has a denominator of 5? Which fraction is larger, 1/2 or 1/4? What is the numerator for the sum of 1/3 + 1/3?*

4. Divide students into groups. Give each group some oranges, plastic knives, and paper plates. Direct the groups to cut three oranges in half. Guide students to combine the orange halves into different groups to indicate various fractions and mixed numbers. For example, students could show that 3/2 is the same as 1 1/2, and 4/2 is the same as 2. Have volunteers write their examples of equivalent fractions on the board.

5. Have students cut three orange halves into thirds. Continue the same process described in Step 4. During independent practice, invite students to cut more oranges into fractional parts, such as fourths, fifths, sixths, and eighths. Have them use these parts to compare fractions and to demonstrate equivalencies.

6. For closure, have each student use orange sections to demonstrate equivalent fractions.

Extended Learning

- Invite students to write recipes for fruit salad. Have them use fractions in the steps for the recipes, such as *Cut a banana into thirds*, or *Mix in 5/8 of an orange*. Have students follow each other's recipes to make the salads.

- Have students make fraction flashcards. On each card, they can draw a shape and divide it into equal sections to indicate different fractions. Students can use their flashcards for practice with fractions or to study for a test.

Round Up: Charts/Posters

Materials

poster board

markers

Skills Objective

Round whole numbers through the millions to the nearest ten, hundred, thousand, ten thousand, and hundred thousand.

The simple act of displaying educational **Charts** and **Posters** in the classroom can support student learning and help students remember concepts. When teaching students about rounding numbers, display a chart in your classroom that they can refer to as they work.

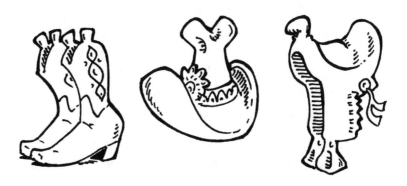

1. Use a poster board and markers to reproduce this flow chart about rounding numbers.

Rounding Numbers

Round 256,499 to the nearest ten thousand.
1. 25<u>6</u>,499
2. 25<u>6</u>,499

   6 > 5
3. 260,000

Find the place to which you are rounding.

Look one place to the right. Is the number 5 or greater than 5?

Round 4,231 to the nearest thousand.
1. <u>4</u>,231
2. 4,<u>2</u>31

   2 < 5
3. 4, 200

If **yes**, add 1 to the place you are rounding.

If **no**, keep the number in the place you are rounding the same.

Change all the numbers to the right of where you are rounding to 0.

2. You may wish to create a second chart to show examples of rounding. Reproduce the following sample to get you started.

Number	Nearest ten	Nearest hundred	Nearest thousand	Nearest ten thousand	Nearest hundred thousand
568	570	600	1000	0	0
3429	3430	3400	3000	0	0
78,261	78,260	78,300	78,000	80,000	0
453,891	453,890	453,900	454,000	450,000	0
8,264,735	8,264,740	8,264,700	8,265,000	8,270,000	8,300,000

Extended Learning

- Have students make their own tables to show how numbers are rounded to the nearest ten, hundred, thousand, ten thousand, and hundred thousand.

- Invite students to draw copies of the flowchart for rounding numbers and put them in their math journals or portfolios.

- Have students write a short paragraph explaining when it might be appropriate to use rounded numbers to solve math problems. For example, shoppers often round to get an estimated cost for items sold by the pound.

Munch a Lunch: Food Web

Materials

Munch a Lunch reproducible

old nature magazines

reference books

construction paper in various colors

scissors

glue

ball

Skills Objectives

Explain how producers and consumers are related to each other within a food chain and food web.

Identify that plants are the primary source of matter and energy in most food chains.

A **Food Web** is a graphic organizer that shows the relationships between various producers and consumers within an ecosystem. In this activity, students work in small groups to research the plant and animal life in a given ecosystem. They then work together to build a food web for their ecosystem.

1. Get students' attention by bouncing a ball in the classroom. Ask: *How do I get the energy to do this?* Lead a discussion about how all living things get energy from food. Without food, living things would not be able to grow, move, or live.

2. Introduce the following vocabulary words:

> **producer:** living thing that produces its own food (a plant)
> **herbivore:** animal that eats only plants (a giraffe)
> **carnivore:** animal that eats other animals (a lion)
> **omnivore:** animal that eats both plants and animals (many birds)

If you like, make a chart to show the vocabulary words, their definitions, and examples.

3. Explain that a food chain shows how different living things get their food. Model for students how to draw a food chain. Draw a tree, a caterpillar, a bird, and a cat. Place an arrow from each food source to its consumer.

4. Point out how most animals eat more than one kind of food and are part of more than one food chain. When there are many connected food chains, a food web is formed.

5. Divide students into small groups. Assign each group a different ecosystem, such as desert, forest, wetland, prairie, mountain, or ocean. Give students a copy of the **Munch a Lunch reproducible (page 31)**.

6. Choose an ecosystem that has not been assigned to model for students how to complete the food web on the reproducible. On the bottom row, list the names of plants in that ecosystem. Above that row, list the names of animals that eat the plants. On the next row, list the animals that eat the animals below. Finally, on the top row, list the animals in the ecosystem that have few, if any, predators.

7. Check to be sure students understand how to use the food web. Invite them to work within their groups to research the plants and animals for their assigned ecosystems and complete their food

webs. Encourage them to use the Internet, encyclopedias, nature magazines, and reference books for their research.

8. Invite students to make posters of their food webs. Give each group a large sheet of construction paper. Have them divide the paper into four sections and cover each section with a different colored strip of construction paper. Have groups print pictures from the Internet of plants and animals they listed on their food web and glue them onto the construction paper strips. Students can also cut pictures out of old nature magazines.

9. Close the activity by having groups present their food webs and posters to the class. Display finished posters on a "world ecosystems" bulletin board.

Extended Learning

- Have students research and create a display of the life cycle of one animal from their food web.

- Encourage students to make a T-chart to compare and contrast the food webs from two different ecosystems.

- Have students write a paragraph describing how a food web might change with the change of seasons.

- Invite students to research how the extinction of one animal in a food web might disrupt that food web. Explore the causes and effects of such a disruption.

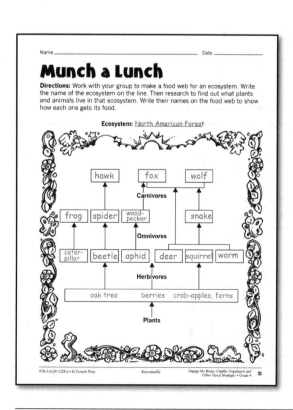

Name _____ Date _____

Munch a Lunch

Directions: Work with your group to make a food web for an ecosystem. Write the name of the ecosystem on the line. Then research to find out what plants and animals live in that ecosystem. Write their names on the food web to show how each one gets its food.

Ecosystem: _____

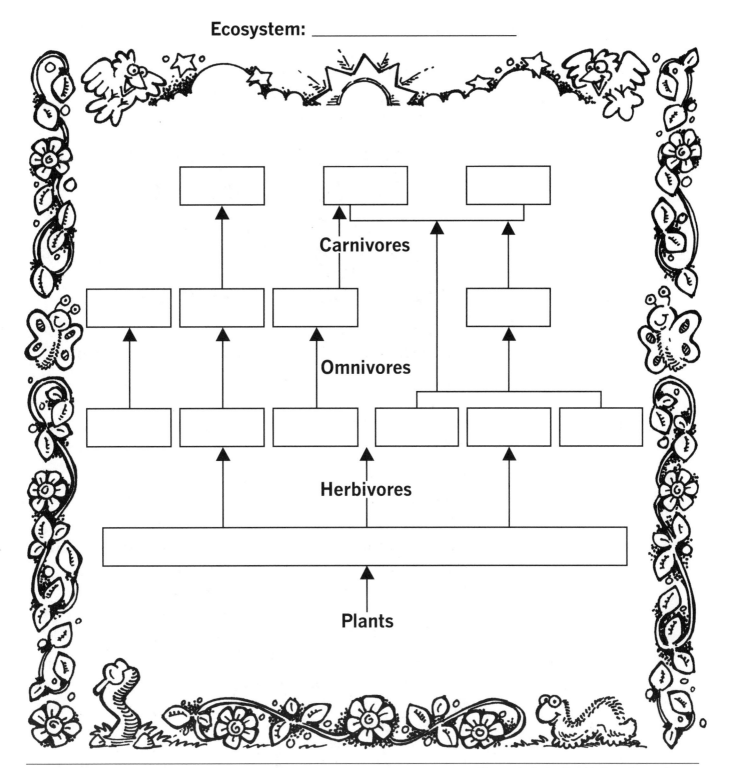

Investigation Station: Scientific Method Diagram

Materials

Investigation Station reproducibles

overhead projector

notebook

reference materials

Skills Objective

Complete a scientific investigation using the steps in the scientific method.

Using a **Diagram** that outlines the steps in the scientific method will help students organize their work during an investigation or experiment. The diagram will prompt them to write a question about a scientific problem, conduct research about their problem, form a hypothesis, develop procedures to test the hypothesis, organize data, and state a conclusion. Because of the many steps involved, you may wish to teach this lesson over the course of several days.

1. Focus students' attention by asking: *How do scientists find answers to questions?* Record all responses on the chalkboard.

2. After discussion, explain that scientists follow a process known as the *scientific method*. By following this process, scientists are able to devise experiments and investigations that are recorded and can be repeated by others.

3. Give students a copy of the **Investigation Station reproducibles (pages 34–36)**. Copy the reproducibles onto overhead transparencies for yourself.

4. Introduce the first step in the process—*Choose a problem*. Have students brainstorm different topics they may wish to explore, and develop a question that can be investigated for each topic. Encourage them to choose topics of interest, to ask questions to which they don't already know the answers, and to choose topics they have the ability to investigate.

5. After brainstorming, model for students how to write a question in the first beaker in the scientific method diagram. Then have students choose their own questions and write them on their diagrams.

6. Work through each step of the scientific method separately. This will probably need to be done over the course of several lessons. Encourage students to use science notebooks to record their research, list their materials and procedures, record and organize their data, and state their conclusions. At each step in the process, model for students what you want them to do and check that they understand. Then have them work independently on their investigations, completing their scientific method diagrams as they work.

7. After the investigations are completed, close the activity by having each student present his or her investigation to the class. Encourage students to use charts, graphs, photographs, and other visual aids for the presentations.

Extended Learning

- Have students work in groups to make posters that illustrate the steps in the scientific process.

- Encourage students to research well-known scientists and write short reports about their discoveries.

- Have students exchange science notebooks and challenge them to repeat each other's investigations by following the procedures listed.

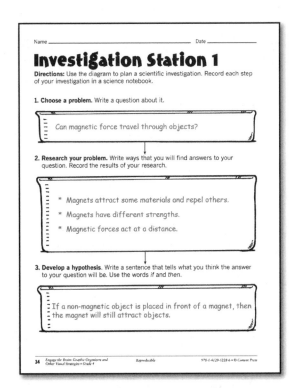

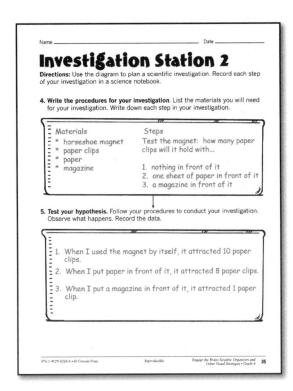

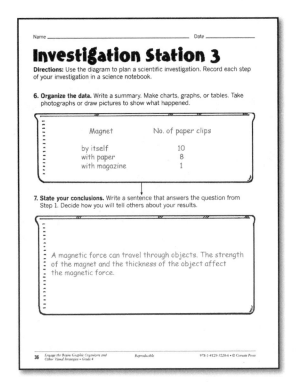

Investigation Station 1

Directions: Use the diagram to plan a scientific investigation. Record each step of your investigation in a science notebook.

1. Choose a problem. Write a question about it.

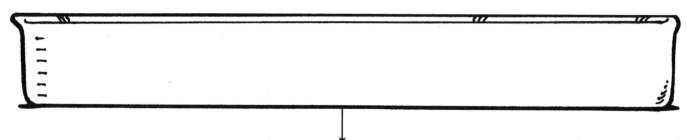

2. Research your problem. Write ways that you will find answers to your question. Record the results of your research.

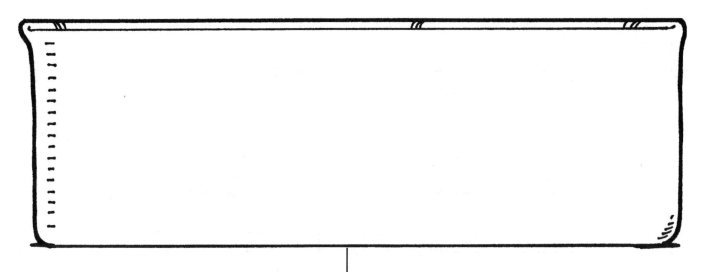

3. Develop a hypothesis. Write a sentence that tells what you think the answer to your question will be. Use the words *if* and *then*.

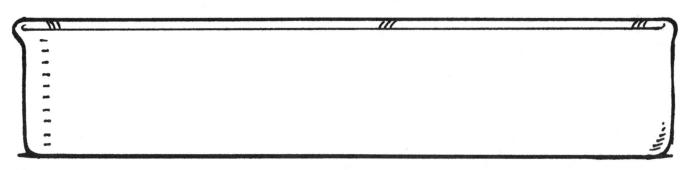

Investigation Station 2

Directions: Use the diagram to plan a scientific investigation. Record each step of your investigation in a science notebook.

4. **Write the procedures for your investigation**. List the materials you will need for your investigation. Write down each step in your investigation.

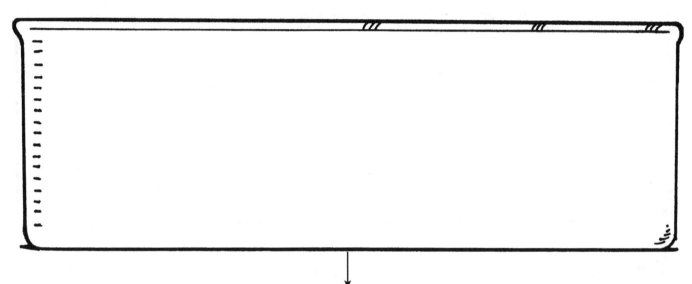

5. **Test your hypothesis.** Follow your procedures to conduct your investigation. Observe what happens. Record the data.

Investigation Station 3

Directions: Use the diagram to plan a scientific investigation. Record each step of your investigation in a science notebook.

6. Organize the data. Write a summary. Make charts, graphs, or tables. Take photographs or draw pictures to show what happened.

7. State your conclusions. Write a sentence that answers the question from Step 1. Decide how you will tell others about your results.

Geology Rocks: Y-Chart

Skills Objectives
Identify different types of rocks.
Compare the characteristics of igneous, sedimentary, and metamorphic rocks.

A **Y-Chart** is used to compare and contrast three different things. The sections of the chart allow students to organize information into distinct categories. In this lesson, students will use a Y-chart to describe the characteristics of the three types of rocks.

Materials
Geology Rocks reproducible

igneous rock samples (granite, basalt, periodite, pumice, obsidian)

sedimentary rock samples (sandstone, limestone, shale, conglomerate, breccia)

metamorphic rock samples (schist, gneiss, slate, quartzite, marble)

magnifying glasses

reference materials

1. Capture students' interest by setting up a discovery table with rock samples. Include samples of igneous rocks, sedimentary rocks, and metamorphic rocks. Stock the table with magnifying glasses, and encourage students to study the rocks independently or with partners.

2. Ask students what they know about how rocks are formed. List all of their ideas on the board, whether they are correct or not.

3. Explain to students that there are three types of rocks—igneous, sedimentary, and metamorphic. Give students a copy of the **Geology Rocks reproducible (page 39)**. Explain that they will use the chart to record how each type of rock is formed and to list examples of each one.

4. Invite volunteers to investigate the formation of igneous rocks. They may look in science textbooks, encyclopedias, on the Internet, or in other available resources. Have volunteers report their findings to the class and model how to record the information on the Y-chart.

5. Check to be sure that everyone understands how to complete the Y-chart before directing students to work independently to learn about the formation of sedimentary and metamorphic rocks. Students may copy the information provided about igneous rocks.

6. When everyone has finished their charts, go back to the information that you listed on the board in Step 2. Challenge students to evaluate each of the ideas and determine which ones are correct. Cross out the incorrect ideas.

Extended Learning

- Have students investigate what different types of rocks are used for. For example, pumice is used in soaps and abrasive cleansers.

- Have students group your rock samples into the three categories. Invite them to use a rock guide to check the accuracy of their work.

- Encourage students to make posters for each type of rock.

- Invite students to bring in found rocks from home or various places such as a park or the beach. Ask the class to explore the rocks and categorize them by type of rock, color, shape, and more.

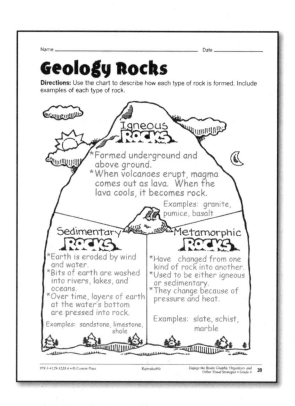

Name _____ Date _____

Geology Rocks

Directions: Use the chart to describe how each type of rock is formed. Include examples of each type of rock.

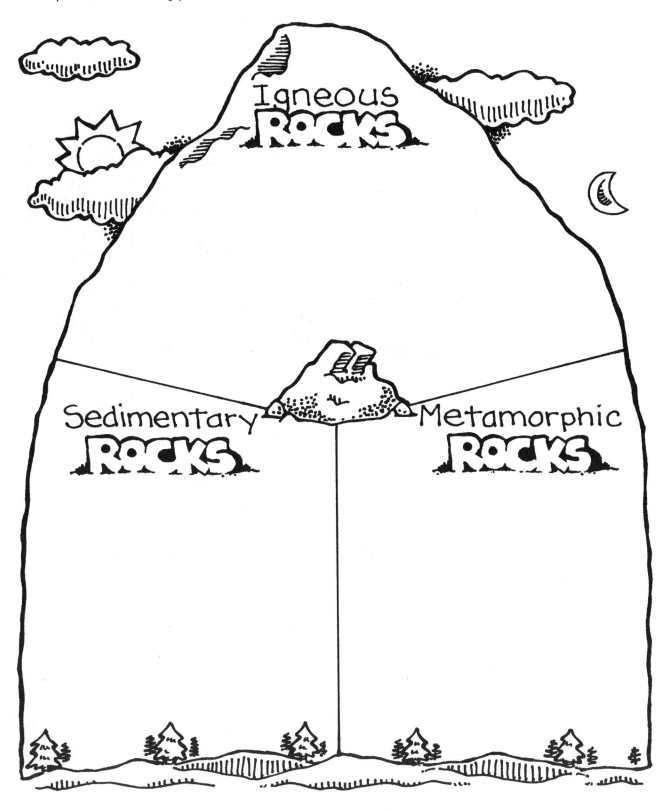

Rock and Roll: Poster

Materials

poster board

construction paper
(red, orange, yellow,
blue, purple, gray)

glue

sand

red paint

paintbrush

Skills Objective

Understand the steps of the rock cycle.

A **Poster** can help students visualize information and make it readily accessible for reference. To help solidify students' understanding of the rock cycle, make a poster to display in your classroom. The poster will show how one type of rock can change into another.

1. Cut nine arrow shapes from different colored construction paper. Make two red arrows and write the word *melting* on each one. Make two orange arrows and write the phrase *heat and pressure* on each one. Make three yellow arrows and write the phrase *erosion caused by wind and water* on each one. Make one light-blue arrow and write the word *cooling* on it. Make one lavender arrow and write the phrase *compacting and cementing* on it.

2. Draw three piles of rocks on gray construction paper. Cut out each rock pile. Label the first rock pile *Igneous Rocks.* Label the second rock pile *Sedimentary Rocks.* Label the third rock pile *Metamorphic Rocks.*

3. Arrange the gray rock-pile shapes and colorful arrows on a poster board and glue them into place.

4. Spread a thin layer of glue between the areas of Igneous Rocks and Sedimentary Rocks. Sprinkle sand over the glue. Write the word *sediments* next to the sand.

5. Use a paintbrush to splatter a small amount of red paint in the area between Metamorphic Rocks and Igneous Rocks. When the paint dries, write the word *magma* next to it.

6. Introduce the poster to students. Explain that the rock cycle is a series of changes that result in rock formation. Under the right conditions, each type of rock can be changed into either of the other two types of rocks. Melting and cooling, heat and pressure, erosion caused by wind and water, and compacting and cementing of sediments are all things that contribute to the formation of rocks.

Extended Learning

- Have students research the formation of one type of rock to create their own diagrams to show the steps in the process.

- Invite students to draw copies of the rock cycle poster in their science journals.

- Have students make flashcards for vocabulary words presented on the rock cycle poster, such as igneous rocks, sedimentary rocks, metamorphic rocks, magma, erosion, compacting, and cementing.

What a Disaster! Fishbone Map

Materials

What a Disaster! reproducible

photographs of areas impacted by natural disasters

science reference books

Skills Objective

Understand the causes of various natural disasters.

A **Fishbone Map** is a type of graphic organizer used to chart many details about a complex topic. Fishbone maps help students visualize information they are learning in a simple, concrete way. In this activity, students investigate the causes of different natural disasters. The fishbone map will help them remain focused on the topic and compare and contrast how different natural disasters occur.

1. Decide ahead of time which four natural disasters you would like students to study. Choose from the following: earthquake, electrical storm, flood, hurricane, monsoon, tornado, tsunami, and volcano. You may wish to focus on natural disasters that occur in your area or on disasters that have had recent news coverage. Write your choices on a copy of the **What a Disaster! reproducible (page 44)**. Write *Causes of Natural Disasters* down the center "spine" of the fishbone map. Then make a copy for each student.

2. Get students instantly hooked on this topic by displaying photographs of areas that have been impacted by natural disasters. Include examples of different disasters such as earthquakes, tsunamis, volcanoes, and floods. Ask students what they think happened in each photograph.

3. Give students a copy of the reproducible. Then divide the class into groups of four. Explain that they will work cooperatively to discover the causes of the natural disasters listed on their papers.

4. Draw a sample fishbone map on the board. Choose a natural disaster that is not listed on students' map and demonstrate how

to complete the fishbone map. List three causes of the natural disaster, one on each "rib" of the map.

5. Check to be sure students understand how to use the graphic organizer before inviting groups to work cooperatively to discover the causes of the natural disasters you have assigned. Circulate around the room to monitor progress, answer questions, and ensure that the graphic organizers are being used correctly.

6. To close the lesson, draw another fishbone map on the board with the same topics you assigned to students. Invite volunteers from each group to come to the board to list the causes for the disasters. Ask students to compare the whole class organizer to the ones they made in their groups and discuss any differences.

Extended Learning

- Have students choose one natural disaster and research it further. Encourage them to create fishbone maps to show the causes, impacts, historical occurrences, and ways to survive the selected disaster.

- Have students locate areas on a map where different natural disasters occur.

- Invite students to make a timeline to show the historical occurrences of one type of natural disaster.

- Have students work in groups to research suggestions for how to survive each type of disaster. Ask each group to create a poster of survival tips to share with the class.

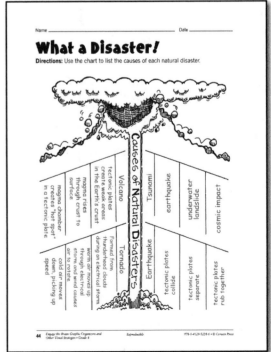

Name _____ Date _____

What a Disaster!

Directions: Use the chart to list the causes of each natural disaster.

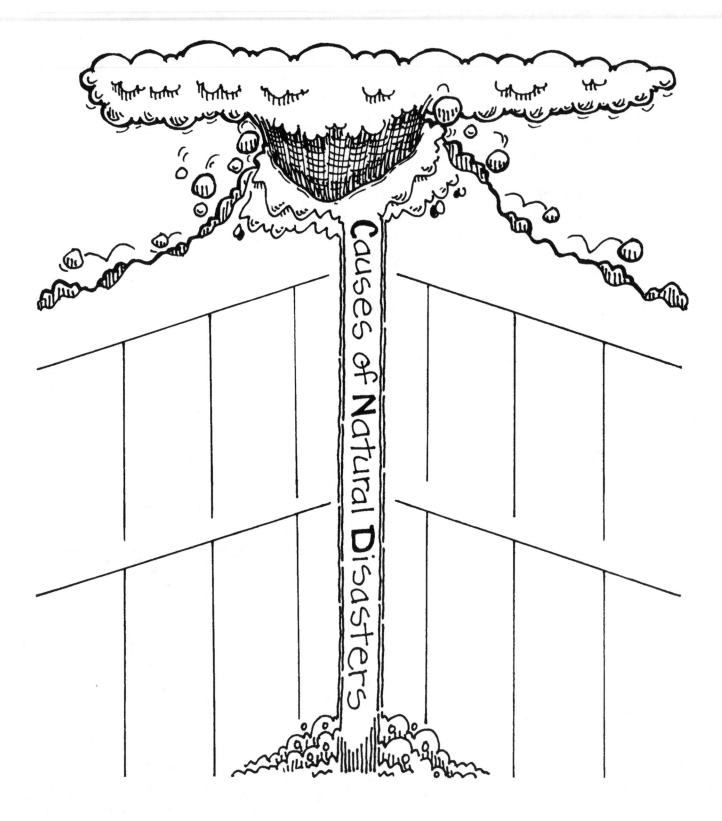

 *Engage the Brain: Graphic Organizers and
Other Visual Strategies • Grade 4*   Reproducible   978-1-4129-5228-6 • © Corwin Press

Beautiful Biomes: Spider Map

Skills Objectives

Identify the plants and animals living within a biome.

Identify the climate associated with a biome.

Identify the specific locations of a type of biome.

A **Spider Map** is a graphic organizer that is useful for listing many details related to a single topic. The spider map format allows for further investigation into each specific detail. In this activity, students will use a spider map graphic organizer in their studies of biomes.

Materials

Beautiful Biomes reproducible

travel magazines and posters that feature various biomes

reference books and magazines about various ecosystems

1. Display travel posters and magazines that feature various biomes around your classroom to get students thinking about the different biomes that make up the earth. Invite students to study the posters and magazines and ask: *In or near which of these places would you most like to live? What plants and animals would you find there? What would the climate be like? In what parts of the world would you find yourself if you lived there?*

2. List these biomes on the board: *taiga (boreal forest), temperate deciduous forest, temperate rain forest, tropical rain forest, tundra, desert, grasslands, rivers and streams, ponds and lakes, wetlands, shorelines, temperate oceans, tropical oceans.*

3. Divide students into groups of two or three. Invite each group to choose one biome to study. Groups will be responsible for presenting reports on the biomes they selected. Each report will focus on the geography of the biome, the climate, and the plants and animals that live there.

4. Give students a copy of the **Beautiful Biomes reproducible (page 47)**. Using the world's largest biome, the taiga (boreal forest), model for students how to complete the spider map graphic organizer. Explain that they will use the map to record notes for their presentations. Point out that they may wish to use sub-categories to further organize their information. For example, under the category of *Animals*, students may wish to include groupings for *herbivores, carnivores,* and *birds of prey.*

5. Check to be sure students understand how to use the graphic organizer before directing groups to conduct research for each topic. As students work, circulate around the room to answer questions and assist as needed.

6. After students have completed their spider maps, invite each group to give a presentation to the class about its biome. You may wish to have students incorporate photographs, charts, and maps into their presentations.

Extended Learning

- Invite students to write creative stories about life in different biomes.

- Have students make a slideshow about their biome on the computer, using a program such as Microsoft® PowerPoint.

- Have students make a landscape painting of their biome.

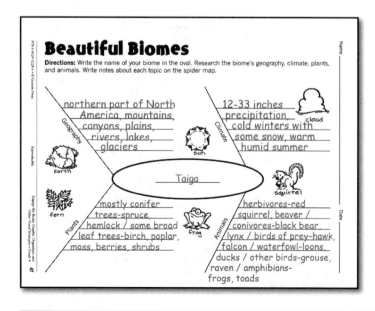

Beautiful Biomes

Directions: Write the name of your biome in the oval. Research the biome's geography, climate, plants, and animals. Write notes about each topic on the spider map.

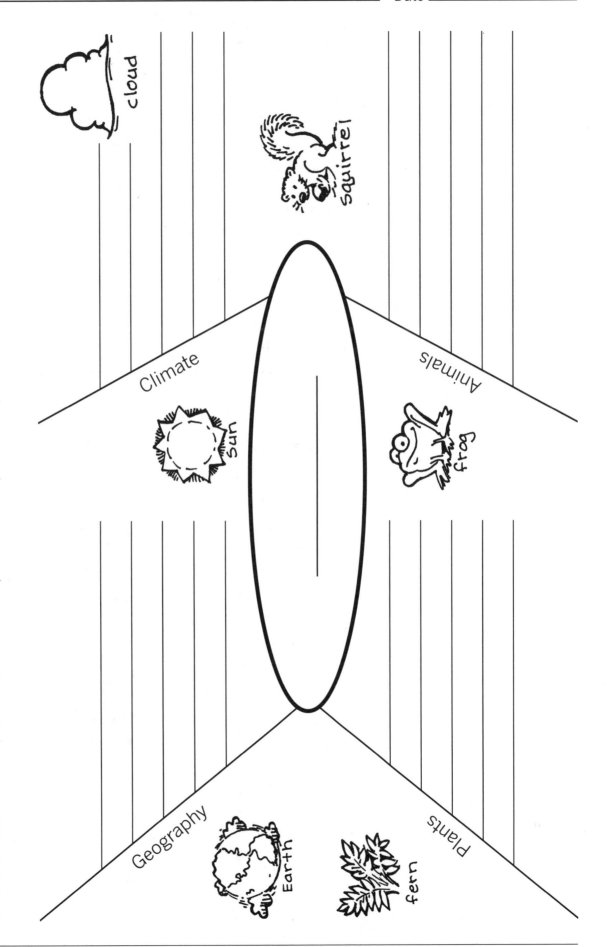

Reproducible   *Engage the Brain: Graphic Organizers and Other Visual Strategies • Grade 4*   **47**

How to Build a Compass: Sequence of Events Chart

Materials

How to Build
a Compass
reproducible

poster board

felt-tipped markers

sewing needles

scissors

pencils

magnets

empty jelly jars

white paper

yarn

tape

Skills Objective

Understand the steps involved in building a simple compass.

A **Sequence of Events Chart** is a visual aid that describes the steps in a process. Using this type of chart allows students to see how one step in a process leads to another and eventually to the outcome. For this activity, you will create a chart to show students how to build a simple compass. Students will follow the instructions on the chart to make their own compasses.

1. Copy the information from the **How to Build a Compass reproducible (page 49)** onto a poster board. Print images of compasses and compass roses from the Internet. Cut out the images and use them to decorate the poster. Display the poster in your science center.

2. Invite students to visit the science center to build their compasses. Before they begin, be sure they understand that they are to follow the instructions on the chart in order.

3. After everyone has had a chance to build their compasses, close the activity with a discussion about how compasses are used.

Extended Learning

- Bring in a variety of compasses for students to examine.

- Take students outside. Have small groups share compasses, and then give them directions to follow, such as: *Take five steps north and three steps east.* Challenge groups to use their compasses to determine which direction they should move.

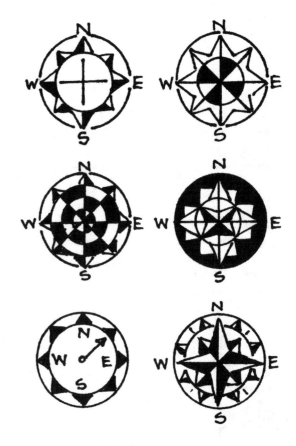

Name _____ Date _____

How to Build a Compass

Directions: Follow these directions to make your own compass.

1. Gather these materials:
- sewing needle
- scissors
- magnet
- empty jelly jar
- pencil
- 2 sheets of white paper
- 6-inch length of yarn
- felt-tipped pen
- tape

2. Magnetize the needle. Hold the needle down with one finger. Stroke the needle with one end of the magnet. Stroke in the same direction several times.

3. Cut a 1-inch square of paper. Push the needle through the paper. The center of the needle should be in the middle of the paper.

4. Make a small hole at the top of the paper. Thread the yarn through the hole. Tie it to the pencil.

5. Rest the pencil across the top of the jelly jar. Let the paper and needle drop down into the jar. (The jar keeps the wind and air from moving the needle.)

6. Use a marker to write the points of a compass on another sheet of paper.

7. Lift the jar and slide the paper underneath it so the **N** on your compass rose lies in the same direction as the pointed end of the needle. Tape the paper in place. Move the jar to different locations and watch how the needle always points north.

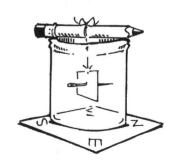

Governments Galore: Chart Matrix

Materials

Governments Galore reproducible

overhead projector

almanac and encyclopedias

Skills Objectives

Compare the similarities and differences between federal, state, and local governments.

Identify how the different levels of government have an impact on our daily lives.

A **Chart Matrix** is a graphic organizer that allows students to organize data related to a variety of topics. In this activity, students use a chart matrix to compare the similarities and differences between federal, state, and local governments.

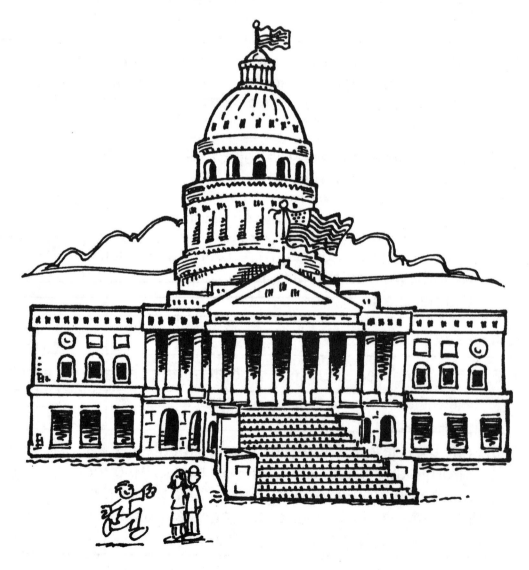

1. Access students' prior knowledge about the duties of governments. On three separate areas of the chalkboard, write *Federal Government*, *State Government*, and *Local Government*. Have students brainstorm things they know about each one and write their responses in the proper areas of the chalkboard.

2. Give students a copy of the **Governments Galore reproducible (page 52)**, and place a transparency of the reproducible on the overhead projector. Use the transparency to demonstrate how to use the chart matrix.

3. Ask students: *Who is the leader of our federal government?* Write the word *president* on the chart and, if you wish, include the current president's name. Continue with the leaders for the state and local governments and other elected officials for all three levels of government.

4. Tell students that they will use encyclopedias, almanacs, and the Internet to learn about how each level of government impacts the areas listed on the chart matrix. Be sure students understand how to complete the chart before directing them to work independently. You may want to direct students to the "How Does Government Affect Me?" lesson at The Democracy Project by PBS Kids at *http://pbskids.org/democracy/mygovt/index.html*.

5. After everyone has completed their charts, call on volunteers to share what they learned. Allow students to copy information from their own charts onto the overhead transparency that you started at the beginning of the lesson. For each category, ask students how their own charts are different from that on the overhead transparency. Encourage students to discuss the different things they learned in their research.

Extended Learning

- Have students choose one category from the chart matrix and write an essay describing how the different levels of government support that function in our society.

- Have students work in groups to write and perform skits about what life would be like if the government did not support these areas of our lives.

- Invite students to hold mock elections for the offices of president, governor, and mayor.

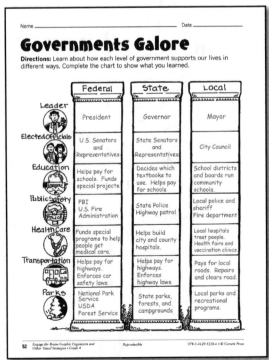

Governments Galore

Directions: Learn about how each level of government supports our lives in different ways. Complete the chart to show what you learned.

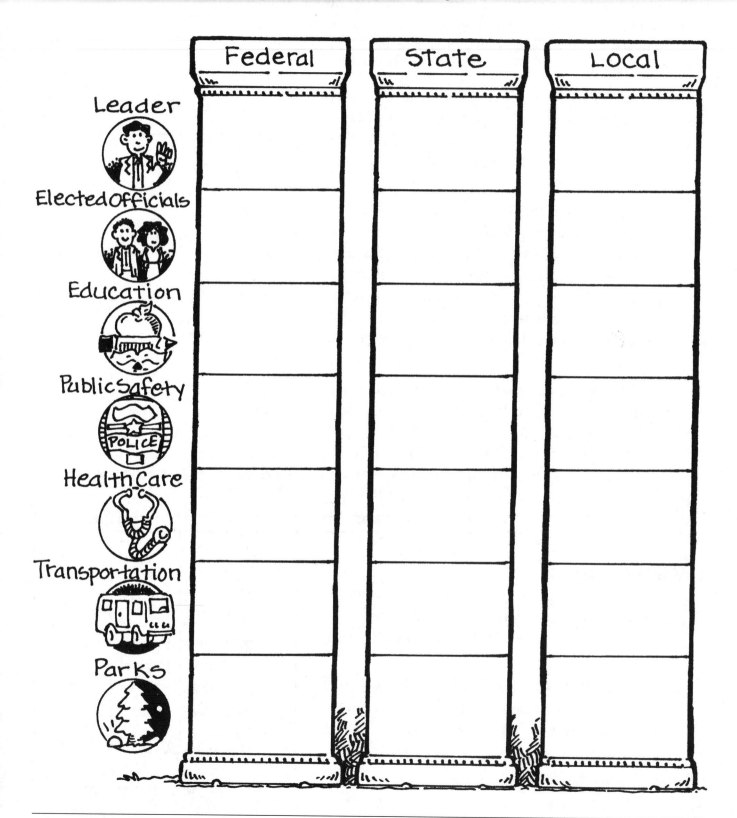

Native Nations: Compare/Contrast Map

Skills Objective

Compare the similarities and differences between major Native American nations.

Materials
Native Nations reproducible

overhead projector

reference books about Native American nations

encyclopedias

A **Compare/Contrast Map** is a graphic organizer that allows students to compare and contrast two concepts according to specific features. In this activity, students study the food, housing, and clothing of a Native American nation from their own state and compare it to another Native American nation from a different region of the country.

1. Engage students' interest by having a brainstorming session about the food, housing, and clothing customs from various cultures in today's world. List students' responses on the board. Point out the similarities and differences of the customs and how they are related to geography.

2. Ask students what they know about a Native American nation from their state. Ask: *How did this nation live before European explorers arrived in North America?* Guide students in a discussion about a local Native American nation's food, housing, and clothing customs, and then compare them to other native nations from North America.

3. Give students a copy of the **Native Nations reproducible (page 55)**, and place a transparency of the reproducible on the overhead. Use the transparency to demonstrate how to complete the graphic organizer.

4. Choose two native nations from different parts of the country, and list their names at the top of the page, such as *Hopi* and *Mohawk*. Write a few examples of how their food was both different and

similar to each other: *Hopi—used dry farming and terrace gardens; Mohawk—hunted deer and elk; Both—farmers grew corn, beans, and squash.* Do the same for housing and clothing.

5. Make sure students understand how to complete the graphic organizer before directing them to work independently. They will compare and contrast a Native American nation from your state and one from another region of the country.

6. Close the activity by having students form discussion groups. Encourage each student to share his or her work with the group. Group members can then compare and contrast all the different nations they researched.

Extended Learning

- Have students make posters showing how different Native Americans lived before the Europeans began exploring North America. Encourage them to include the types of food they ate, the houses they lived in, and the clothes they wore.

- Have students write fictional diary entries as if they were members of a Native American nation prior to the European exploration of North America.

- Encourage students to read biographies of famous Native Americans, such as Maria Tallchief and Sitting Bull.

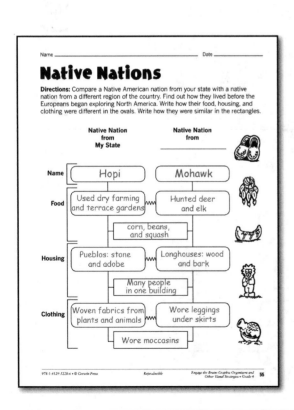

Native Nations

Directions: Compare a Native American nation from your state with a native nation from a different region of the country. Find out how they lived before the Europeans began exploring North America. Write how their food, housing, and clothing were different in the ovals. Write how they were similar in the rectangles.

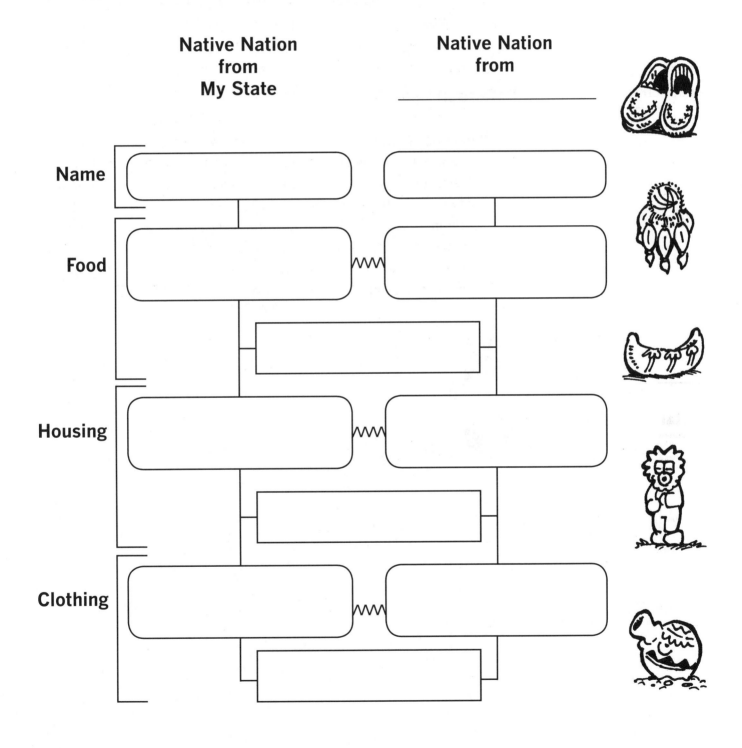

Native Nation from My State

Native Nation from _____

Name

Food

Housing

Clothing

Comparing Lives: Triple Venn Diagram

Materials

Comparing Lives
reproducible

social studies
textbook

reference books
about your state's
history

encyclopedias

Skills Objectives

Describe the daily lives of people who lived in your state in the 1800s.
Compare and contrast three different groups of people.

A **Triple Venn Diagram** is a graphic organizer that allows students to
compare and contrast three different items or subjects. The overlapping
circles are used to indicate traits that the different subjects have in
common. The parts of the circles that do not overlap are used to show
the traits that are unique to each subject. In this activity, students select
three groups of people who lived in their state during the 1800s. They
will use a triple Venn diagram to show the similarities and differences
between the groups.

1. Introduce students to the triple Venn diagram by drawing a diagram
   on the board. Draw and label a row of shapes as shown in the
   illustration. Ask students to identify which shape is a circle but is
   not small or shaded (Circle F). Write the letter *F* in the part of the
   diagram marked *Circle* that does not overlap with any other part of
   the diagram. Continue with the rest of the shapes until each one is
   properly placed on the diagram. (Note: Shape B is the only shape
   that does not match any of the criteria on the diagram.)

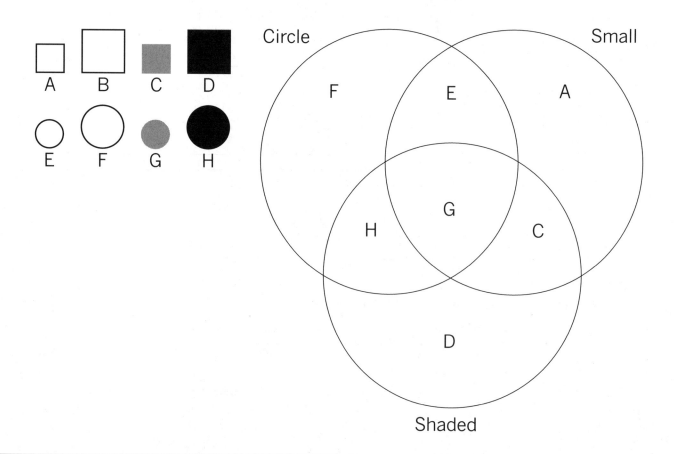

2. Give students a copy of the **Comparing Lives reproducible (page 58)**. Explain that they will select three groups of people who lived in their state during the 1800s. As a group, brainstorm a list of possibilities. Then invite students to choose the groups they wish to learn about and write their names on the lines around the Venn diagram.

3. Draw another triple Venn diagram on the board and model for students how to use it to compare three sets of people, such as *Plantation Owners, Slaves,* and *Overseers.*

4. Be sure students understand how to complete the diagram before directing them to work independently. Encourage students to use their social studies textbooks, encyclopedias, and other reference books to learn more about the groups they are studying.

5. Encourage each student to display his or her work on a bulletin board. Use the bulletin board as a social studies center, and invite students to visit the center when they have finished other work.

Extended Learning

- Invite students to work in small groups to write skits that demonstrate the daily lives of different groups of people.

- Have students make a graphic organizer to show how life today compares to life in the 1800s.

- Have students write short reports about the daily life of one group of people in the 1800s.

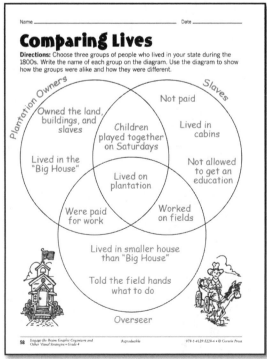

Comparing Lives

Directions: Choose three groups of people who lived in your state during the 1800s. Write the name of each group on the diagram. Use the diagram to show how the groups were alike and how they were different.

Nifty Notes: Thematic Map

Skills Objectives
Identify the main idea, subtopics, and supporting details in a reading passage.
Take notes while reading a text.

Materials

Nifty Notes reproducible

social studies textbook

overhead projector

small rubber ball

A **Thematic Map** is a graphic organizer used to outline information from a text. In this activity, students use a thematic map while reading a chapter from their social studies textbook. They will begin by identifying the main idea of the chapter and writing a topic sentence. Then, they will add subtopics and supporting details to their maps.

1. Invite students to sit in a circle. Then review a chapter from your social studies textbook that students have already read.

2. Toss a small rubber ball to one student in the circle. Have him or her identify the main idea of that chapter, and then toss the ball to another student. The second student then identifies one subtopic of the main idea. He or she tosses the ball to another student who then provides a supporting detail for the subtopic. Have students continue to toss the ball around the circle, providing subtopics and supporting details for the chapter's main idea.

3. Have students return to their desks, and give them a copy of the **Nifty Notes reproducible (page 61)**. Place a transparency of the reproducible on the overhead. Have students open their social studies textbooks to the chapter you reviewed in Step 1.

4. Demonstrate for students how to use the thematic map to take notes about the chapter. Write a topic sentence in the Main Idea box on the transparency. Call on volunteers to identify three subtopics, and record them in the circles. Then ask volunteers to

name three supporting details for each subtopic, and write them in the rectangles.

5. Assign students a new chapter to read in their social studies textbooks. Check to see that they understand how to complete the thematic map before directing them to take notes on the chapter as they read independently. If you wish, you may direct students to take notes on smaller sections of the chapter.

6. After everyone has completed their work, allow a few volunteers to share their thematic maps with the class. Invite students to share all of their ideas for a class thematic map.

7. Give students several copies of the thematic maps to keep in their desks. They can use them to take notes on future readings across the curriculum. These maps work well to review information for a report or as a study aid for tests.

Extended Learning

- Have students create storyboards to illustrate the concepts in the textbook chapter.

- Write main ideas on flashcards, and have students name subtopics and supporting details for each one.

- Have students use a thematic map for a character study of an historical figure featured in their textbooks.

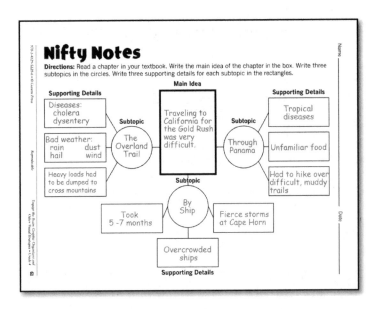

Name _____ Date _____

Nifty Notes

Directions: Read a chapter in your textbook. Write the main idea of the chapter in the box. Write three subtopics in the circles. Write three supporting details for each subtopic in the rectangles.

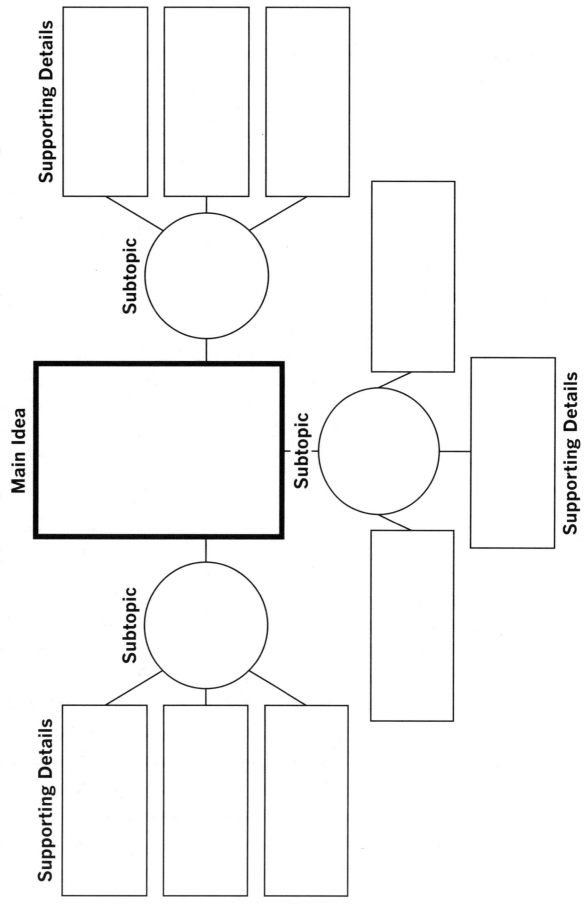

Main Idea

Subtopic

Supporting Details

Supporting Details

Supporting Details

Our History: Timeline

Materials

butcher paper

markers

social studies textbook

Skills Objective

Comprehend the sequence of historical events.

A **Timeline** is a visual aid that lets students see how events in history relate to one another. The events are shown chronologically over a period of time. Start creating this visual aid at the beginning of the school year and continue adding to it throughout the year.

1. Ahead of time, cut a 36-inch sheet of butcher paper for each century of history you will study. You may wish to use a few different colors to help distinguish between each century.

2. Divide each sheet of paper into three 1/2-inch segments, one for each decade. Label the segments with the range of years that they represent. For example, *1901–1910, 1911–1920, 1921–1930,* and so on.

3. Staple the sheets of butcher paper to the walls of your classroom in sequential order. Hang the paper low enough on the wall so students can help you add information to the timeline.

4. Throughout the year, add important events in history to the timeline. Label each event with the year that it occurred. Invite students to help create the timeline as they read about history in their social studies textbooks.

Extended Learning

- Have students make timelines of their own personal histories or of their family histories.

- Invite students to research events in history that are related to specific topics that interest them, such as sports or music. Invite them to add information to the class timeline about their topics.

- Have students write newspaper articles about events shown on the timeline.

Know the Facts: T-Chart

Materials

Know the Facts
reproducible

social studies
textbook

newspapers

highlighter pens

Skills Objective

Identify the difference between facts and opinions.

A **T-Chart** enables students to list information about two topics or ideas, and then visually compare, contrast, and clarify the material. Ideas may be examined in a variety of ways, such as: pros and cons, advantages and disadvantages, causes and effects, problems and solutions, or facts and opinions. In this activity, students learn that a fact is something that is true and can be checked or proven. They also learn that an opinion is something that one person believes is true but that others may disagree with. The T-chart will help them compare facts and opinions.

1. Introduce students to this activity by writing three statements on the board. The first statement should be a fact, such as: *In the early 1900s, many children worked 15 hours a day at dangerous jobs in mills, factories, and canneries.* The next two statements should be two different opinions about the fact, such as: *Children from poor families should work to help support their families* and *All children under 16 years old should go to school instead of working to support their families.*

2. Ask students to identify which statement is a fact and which two are opinions.

3. Draw a simple T-chart on the board. Label one column *Facts*, and label the other column *Opinions*. Have students skim

through a chapter of their social studies textbook. Invite them to take turns reading aloud statements and determining if the statements are facts or opinions. Model how to record the statements on your T-chart.

4. Give each student two different colored highlighter pens, a copy of the **Know the Facts reproducible (page 66)**, and a section of the local newspaper. Have students read an article from the newspaper and highlight facts with one color and opinions with another color.

5. Make sure everyone understands how to complete the T-chart before directing them to copy the newspaper article statements into the appropriate columns.

6. Close the activity by having students share one factual statement and one opinion from the articles they read.

Extended Learning

- Have students use facts to write a persuasive newspaper article about a topic that is important to them.

- Discuss with students how the media uses both facts and opinions to influence how people feel about current issues.

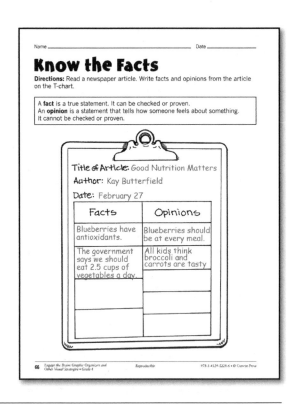

Know the Facts

Directions: Read a newspaper article. Write facts and opinions from the article on the T-chart.

A **fact** is a true statement. It can be checked or proven.
An **opinion** is a statement that tells how someone feels about something.
It cannot be checked or proven.

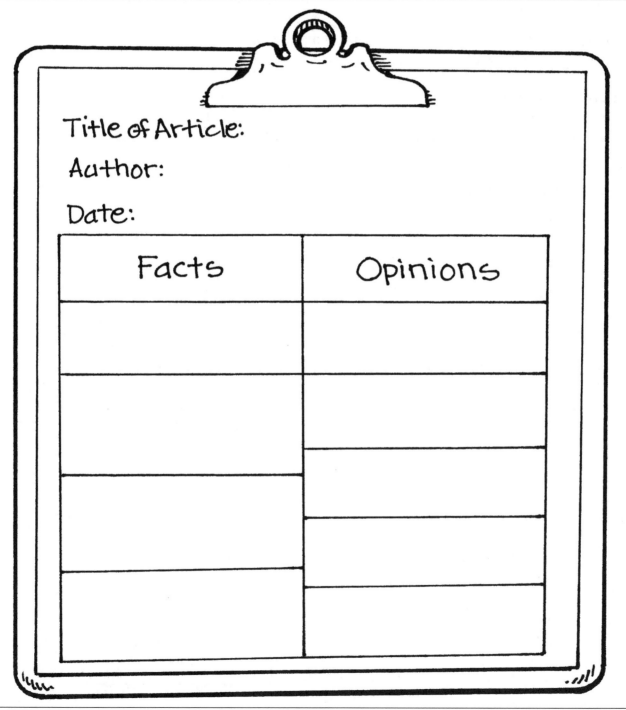

Title of Article:

Author:

Date:

Facts	Opinions

Name That Term: Picture Glossary

Skills Objective
Increase knowledge of geographic terminology.

Materials

Name That Term
reproducible

poster board

scissors

glue

A **Picture Glossary** links vocabulary words and their definitions with concrete images to help increase understanding and memory. In this activity, you will create a wall-sized picture glossary of geographic terms, and students will have the opportunity to make a desk-sized version.

1. Use the Internet to collect images of the geographic terms listed in the chart. As often as possible, use photographic images of real places. The Google™ search engine has an extensive collection of images available, many of which can be printed for free.

2. Once you have printed your images, cut them out and glue them to sheets of poster board. Write the matching geographic term and definition next to each image. You may also wish to show how the term would be used in a sentence. Display the picture glossary on the wall as a visual aid.

3. If you would like students to create a desk-sized version of the glossary, give each student five copies of the **Name That Term reproducible (page 69)**. Have students copy the terms and definitions from your wall glossary and collect their own images to match.

Geographic Terms

basin: bowl-shaped area of land that is lower than the land surrounding it

bay: part of a sea, ocean, or lake that extends into the land

cliff: steep, almost vertical, or overhanging face of a hill, mountain, or plain

coast: land near a shore

desert: dry area of land where there is little plant life

glacier: large body of ice that moves slowly down a mountain or over land

harbor: sheltered body of water where boats and ships can safely dock

hill: raised and rounded mass of land, smaller than a mountain

island: body of land completely surrounded by water

isthmus: narrow strip of land connecting two larger land areas

lake: body of water completely surrounded by land

mesa: wide, flat-topped mountain with steep sides

mountain: great mass of land that rises high above the surrounding land

---

mountain pass: gap between mountains

mountain range: series of mountains

ocean: salty body of water that covers most of Earth's surface

peninsula: piece of land, connected to the mainland, that juts out into the water

plain: wide, flat area of land

prairie: large, flat area of grassland that has no trees

river: large stream of water

sea level: level of the surface of the ocean

strait: narrow channel of water that connects two larger bodies of water

tree line: on a mountain, the area above which no trees grow

valley: low land between hills or mountains

volcano: opening in the earth, often part of a mountain, through which lava and gasses escape

glacier

mountains

volcano

Extended Learning

- Encourage students to draw maps that include some of the geographic terms used in this activity.

- Have students identify the types of land and water forms found in their community.

- Have students work in small groups to compile lists of supplies that would be needed if they were to spend one week living on a mountain, in a desert, and on the open ocean.

Name That Term

Directions: Make a picture glossary of geography terms. Write the terms and definitions on the lines. Glue a photograph or draw a picture in the box to match each term.

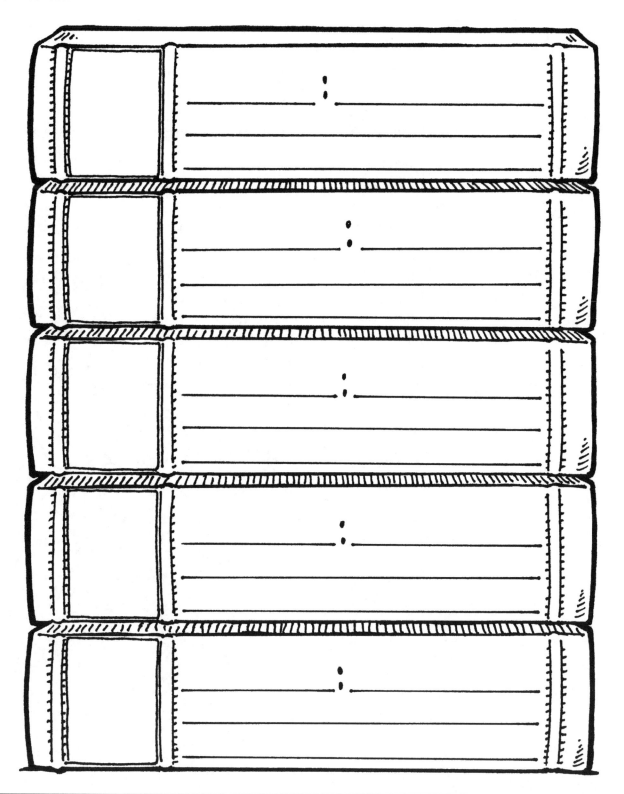

CHAPTER 4

Language Arts

Wonderful Words: Vocabulary Web

Materials

Wonderful Words
reproducible

overhead projector

dictionary

thesaurus

Skills Objectives

Use a dictionary to determine the meanings of words and identify their parts of speech.

Use a thesaurus to determine related words and concepts.

Expand reading vocabulary.

Write sentences to demonstrate comprehension of vocabulary words.

A **Vocabulary Web** allows students to organize and process information related to words they are learning and studying. In this activity, students use a vocabulary web to record a new word, write its definition and part of speech, list three synonyms and three antonyms, and use the word in a sentence.

1. Get students warmed up for this activity by playing a "word scavenger hunt" with them. Give each student a dictionary and a thesaurus. Then direct students to search for words based on criteria you present. For example: *Find an antonym for the word* **reflect**. *Find an adverb that begins with the letter* **s**.

2. Give students a copy of the **Wonderful Words reproducible (page 72)**, and place a transparency of the reproducible on the overhead projector. Choose a vocabulary word from a text you are reading with your class and write it in the word box. Ask student volunteers to provide you with the word's part of speech and

definition, three synonyms and three antonyms, and a sentence using the word. Demonstrate how to fill in the information on the transparency.

3. Be sure that students understand how to complete the vocabulary web before directing them to complete it independently. Invite them to choose words that are unfamiliar from a text they are reading. Have each student complete a vocabulary web for the word he or she chooses.

4. Keep a supply of vocabulary webs available. Assign students the task of completing one new web each day. Invite them to staple their webs together to create personal dictionaries.

5. Close the activity by having students tell the class which words they chose and the synonyms or antonyms that go with the words.

Extended Learning

- Have students make flashcards of the words used on their vocabulary maps.

- Collect the vocabulary maps and use the words for a class game of charades.

- Before transitioning from one activity to another, have students name a word, along with a synonym and an antonym.

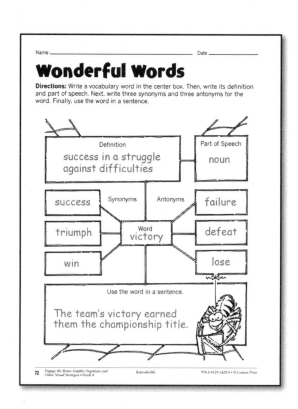

Wonderful Words

Directions: Write a vocabulary word in the center box. Then, write its definition and part of speech. Next, write three synonyms and three antonyms for the word. Finally, use the word in a sentence.

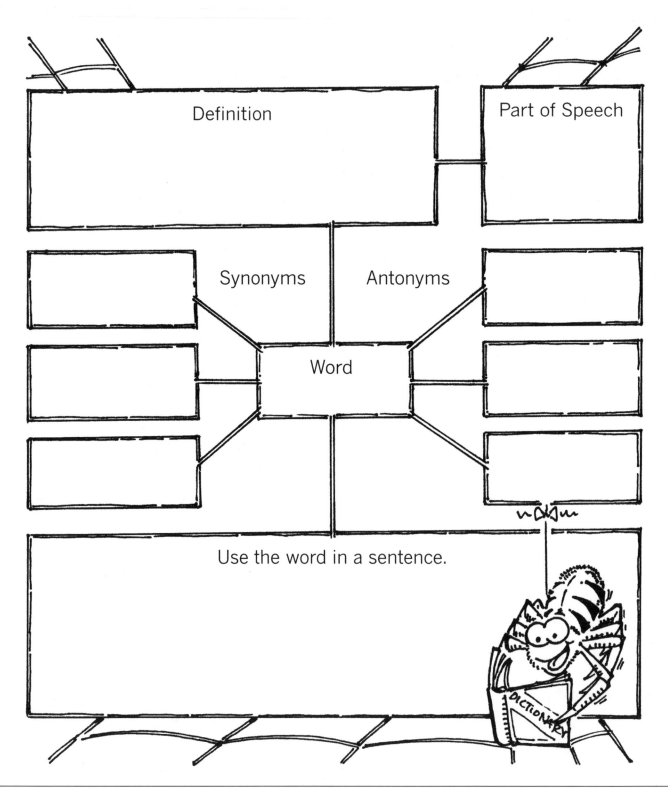

Definition

Part of Speech

Synonyms   Antonyms

Word

Use the word in a sentence.

Reproducible   978-1-4129-5228-6 • © Corwin Press

Flower Power: Story Map

Skills Objectives
Identify the elements of a story.
Define the overall theme of a story.

Materials
Flower Power reproducible

overhead projector

A **Story Map** is a graphic organizer that helps students analyze a story. Using a story map allows students to identify the important elements of a story, including the characters, setting, problem, and solution. They also have the opportunity to express the overall theme, or lesson, of the story. In this activity, students will complete a story map after reading a story of their choice.

1. Introduce this lesson by reviewing a number of books that students have already read. Display the books along the rail of the chalkboard. Think of one sentence that describes the theme of each book and say it aloud. Challenge students to match the theme with the appropriate book. For example, you could say that the theme for Eve Bunting's *Nasty, Stinky Sneakers* is, "It is unfair to win a contest by cheating."

2. After identifying the theme for each of the books you displayed, choose one book to use for a model on how to complete a story map. Copy the **Flower Power reproducible (page 75)** onto a transparency and place it on the overhead projector.

3. Point out each section of the flower graphic organizer, and ask students to identify the characters, setting, problem, and solution for the book you chose. Demonstrate how to write the information on the map.

4. Give each student a copy of the Flower Power Story Map reproducible. Tell them they will use the story map to write about the elements of a book of their choosing or one they read in class. Check to make sure they understand how to use the story map before they begin independent work.

5. Close the activity by having students group themselves by the books they chose. Have each group present their story maps to the class.

Extended Learning

- Have students draw a comic strip version of the stories they read.

- Encourage students to make shoe box dioramas to illustrate important scenes from their books.

- Have students choose a theme and write a short story to go with it.

- Invite students to change one element of their story, such as setting, solution, or problem. Then have them complete another story map to show how the story changes.

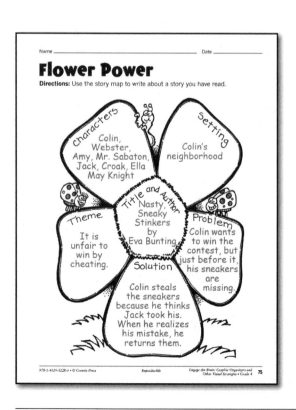

Name _____ Date _____

Flower Power

Directions: Use the story map to write about a story you have read.

Characters
Colin, Webster, Amy, Mr. Sabaton, Jack, Croak, Ella May Knight

Setting
Colin's neighborhood

Title and Author
Nasty, Sneaky Stinkers by Eva Bunting

Theme
It is unfair to win by cheating.

Problem
Colin wants to win the contest, but just before it, his sneakers are missing.

Solution
Colin steals the sneakers because he thinks Jack took his. When he realizes his mistake, he returns them.

Name _____   Date _____

Flower Power

Directions: Use the story map to write about a story you have read.

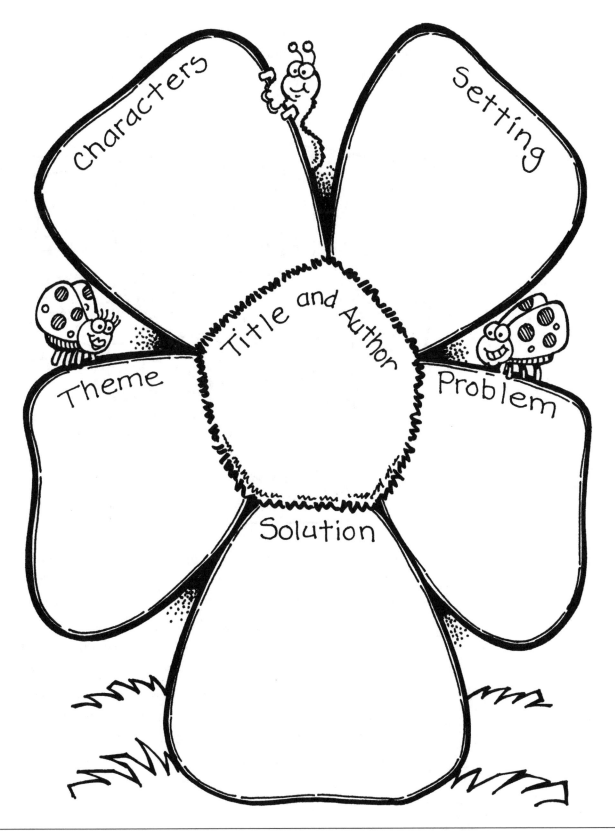

One Thing Leads to Another: Action/Reaction Map

Skills Objective

Distinguish between cause and effect in a story.

An **Action/Reaction Map** is a graphic organizer that helps students identify cause-and-effect relationships. In this activity, students read works of fiction, look for actions that cause reactions, and record them on the map.

1. Get students' attention by displaying a photograph of some people engaged in an activity. For example, you might show a photo of a baseball team celebrating a victory. Ask students what the people in the photo are doing (*cheering*) and why they are doing it (*because they won the game*). Display several photos and ellicit from students the possible causes and effects of the scenes.

2. Give students a copy of the **One Thing Leads to Another reproducible (page 78)**, and place a transparency of the reproducible on the overhead. Model for students how to complete the action/reaction map by working through a story they have recently read.

3. Have students begin by choosing a character from the story, such as *Amber Brown*. Then have them identify a problem the character has and the action the character takes. Write students' responses on the transparency. Next, record reactions caused by the character's action and any subsequent actions that result.

4. Confirm that students understand how to complete the action/ reaction map before having them choose a reading selection and complete the map independently. Circulate around the room as students work, answering questions and giving guidance as needed.

5. Close the activity by having students draw a series of pictures to illustrate the actions and reactions that they wrote about. They can draw in storyboard or comic book style.

Extended Learning

- Have students draw pictures on index cards that show cause and effect. For example, one picture can show a child tripping on a curb (the cause) and the matching picture can show that child dropping his ice cream cone (the effect). Collect all the cards and have students use them to play a memory match game.

- Have students write cause-and-effect statements that focus on feelings. For example, When I take out the trash, it makes my dad feel happy. They can write one half of the sentence on one index card and the other half on another index card. Place all the sentence parts in a shoebox. Invite students to match the sentence parts in their free time.

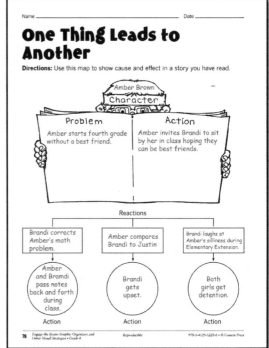

One Thing Leads to Another

Directions: Use this map to show cause and effect in a story you have read.

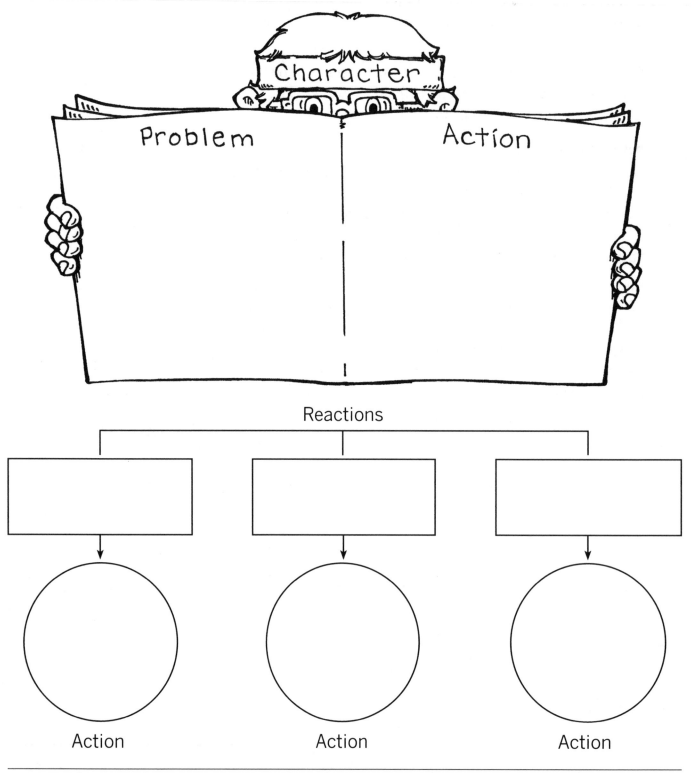

State Your Case: Writing Chart

Skills Objectives
Write a multiple-paragraph composition organized around a central theme.
Write an introductory paragraph with a topic sentence.
Include supporting paragraphs with simple facts and details.
Summarize the points made in the composition with a concluding paragraph.

Materials
State Your Case reproducible

overhead projector

A **Writing Chart** can help students plan what they want to say in a multiple-paragraph composition. This chart provides a place to write a topic sentence and jot notes for the supporting paragraphs and the conclusion. In this activity, students use a writing chart in pre-writing exercises for developing persuasive arguments.

1. Get students focused on this activity by asking: *What is something that you want to do or want to have that your parents won't allow?* List students' responses on the board.

2. Tell students that developing a clear and logical case for what you want can help convince people to at least consider the idea. Tell students that a persuasive argument explains to someone what you want and provides details and facts to support the argument.

3. Give students a copy of the **State Your Case reproducible (page 81)**, and place a transparency of the reproducible on the overhead projector. Choose one of the topics students mentioned in Step 1 and use it to model how to plan an essay. For example: *I want to go to soccer camp.*

4. Ask volunteers to present a topic sentence for the introductory paragraph. For example: *This summer, I want to go to a sleep-away soccer camp.* Then list the main topic for each paragraph. For example: *Soccer camp is fun. Soccer camp is educational. I can help pay for camp.*

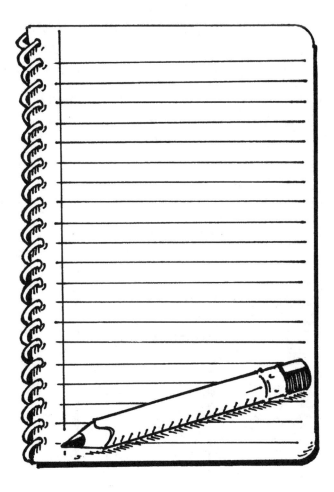

5. Each topic will need three supporting details to support the main idea. Write their ideas on the transparency. Finally, write a sentence that summarizes the ideas on the chart in the *Conclusion* box.

6. Bring students' attention to their State Your Case reproducible. Tell them to choose a topic for a persuasive essay and use the chart to plan it. Make sure students understand how to use the writing chart before inviting them to work independently.

7. When students are finished with their charts, encourage them to share their arguments with partners to get feedback. Then invite students to write a three-paragraph essay based on their charts.

8. Close the activity by inviting each student to read his or her essay aloud to the class. Ask the class to vote on which students' essays were the most persuasive, and why.

Extended Learning

- Have students work in small groups to offer critiques of the essays. Encourage students to make revisions based on the critiques.

- Have students work in teams to debate a topic. Have one group present arguments for the pro side of the debate and have the other group present arguments for the con side.

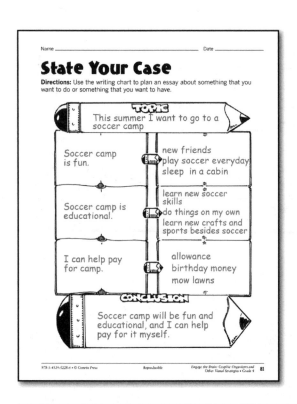

State Your Case

Directions: Use the writing chart to plan an essay about something that you want to do or something that you want to have.

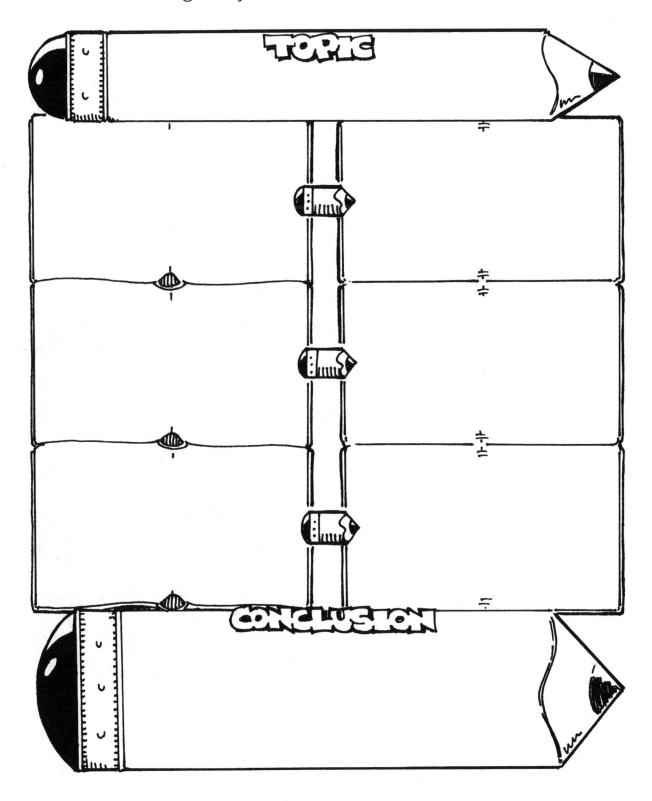

Rocking Reports: Cluster Map

Materials

Rocking Reports reproducible

overhead projector

reference materials

Skills Objectives

Use brainstorming techniques to develop topics for an informational report.
Use various reference materials to aid writing.
Write an informational report.

A **Cluster Map** is used to help students generate ideas about a specific topic. In this activity, students select a topic and use reference materials to learn more about it. After some research, students use the cluster map to record their ideas about the topic and then write informational reports.

1. Introduce this activity by helping students brainstorm a list of topics that they would like to know more about. List their ideas on the board. Invite each student to select one idea.

2. Tell students that they will write informational reports about the topics they selected. Give students some time to do preliminary research on their topics. Give students the opportunity to visit the school library to gather resources and search the Internet for student-friendly articles.

3. Show students how to use a cluster map to gather ideas for their reports. Give them a copy of the **Rocking Reports reproducible (page 84)**, and place a transparency of the reproducible on the overhead projector. Model for students how to complete the chart using the transparency.

4. Choose a topic that students already know about, such as *Getting Fit*, and write it in the center circle on the transparency. Ask students to identify four supporting topics and write them in the ovals. For example: *Flexibility, Strength Training, Endurance,* and *Aerobic Exercise.* Continue by writing details for each supporting topic in the squares.

5. Call students' attention to their Rocking Reports reproducible. Make sure students understand how to use the cluster map. Encourage them to use the research they have already completed to generate ideas for their reports. Have students write their ideas on the cluster map.

6. When students have completed their cluster maps, have them write the first drafts of their informational reports. Encourage students to share their drafts in small groups, make revisions, and then publish a final draft. Compile the final drafts into a class book, and encourage students to read the book during free time.

Extended Learning

- Have students prepare charts, graphs, and other visual aids to incorporate into their reports.

- Encourage students to give oral presentations of their reports.

- Have students write mini quizzes to use with their reports. Challenge students to read each report and then test their knowledge of the topic by taking the quiz.

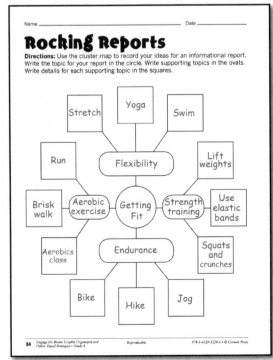

Rocking Reports

Directions: Use the cluster map to record your ideas for an informational report. Write the topic for your report in the circle. Write supporting topics in the ovals. Write details for each supporting topic in the squares.

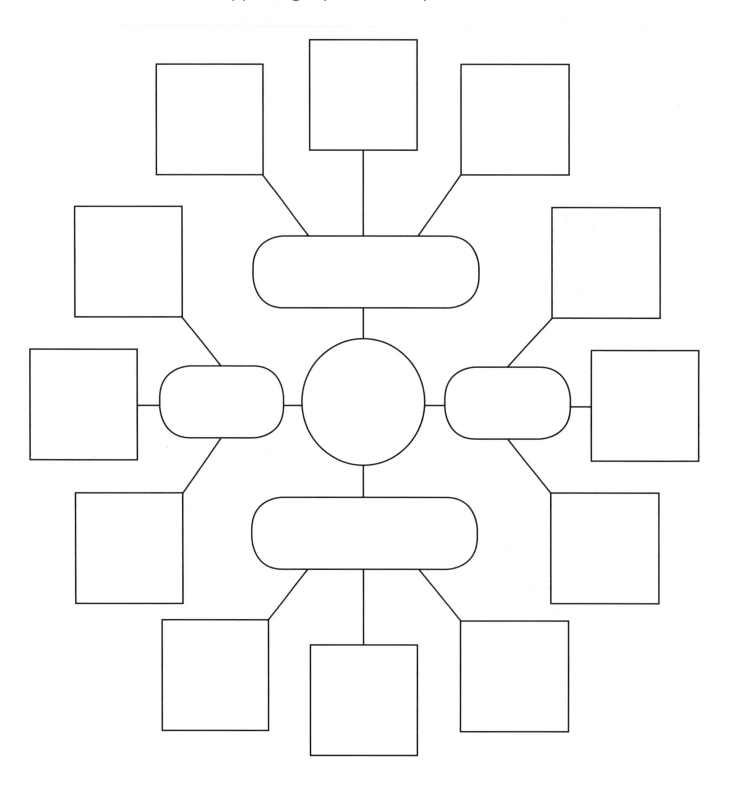

Say, "Cheese!" Bulletin Board Display

Skills Objective
Learn and apply the rules for capitalization.

Materials
bulletin board

art supplies

camera

Having students assist you in creating a **Bulletin Board Display** can support student learning as well as help to reinforce important concepts. In this activity, the rules for capitalization are printed and used as banners on a bulletin board. Students then use photographs to illustrate each rule.

1. Use a computer and printer to make a banner for each capitalization rule listed in the box. Invite students to decorate the printed banners using a variety of art supplies.

Capitalization Rules

Begin every sentence with a capital letter.

Begin the names of people with a capital letter.

Begin the names of places with a capital letter.

Begin the names of streets, cities, counties, states, and countries with a capital letter.

Begin the names of organizations with a capital letter.

Begin titles of books, newspapers, and magazines with a capital letter.

Begin titles of songs, musical compositions, and works of art with a capital letter.

---

2. Arrange the banners on a bulletin board. Leave ample space in between each banner to display photographs.

3. Divide the class into small groups. Invite one group at a time to use a camera to take pictures of different items that represent each rule. For example, students can take pictures of a name placard on a desk, a street sign, and the front page of a newspaper.

4. Invite each group to attach their photographs to the appropriate section of the bulletin board.

Extended Learning

- Type a brief story or passage without using any capitalization. Challenge students to correct every capitalization error in the text.

- Have students list the capital letters in a column down one side of a sheet of paper. Then set a timer for three minutes and challenge them to write as many first names as they can for each letter before the timer goes off. Reward a small prize to the student who writes the most names with proper capitalization.

- Place large self-stick notes on the inside front covers of several books. Encourage students to write new titles for the books on the notes.

The Writing Process: Poster

Skills Objective
Understand the stages of the writing process.

Students often feel that once they complete the first draft of a writing assignment, their work is finished. They need to learn that writing is a process that includes several valuable steps on the way to a finished product. Post an educational **Poster** in the classroom to help students see that many steps are involved in creating a quality finished writing piece.

Materials
The Writing Process reproducible

poster board

colored paper

art supplies

1. Use a computer and printer or a variety of art supplies to make an attention-grabbing poster to display in your classroom. Include the information shown on **The Writing Process reproducible (page 88)**. Be sure to use a large, easy-to-read font. If you wish, print or write each step on different-colored paper.

2. Cut out the blocks of type and arrange them in order on a sheet of poster board. Glue them in place.

3. Give students a copy of The Writing Process reproducible to keep in their writing folders. They can use the reproducible to remind them of the steps they need to take each time they write an essay, report, or other writing piece.

Extended Learning
- Have students form small critique groups for their writing. Remind students to offer helpful suggestions and deserving praise during the critiques.

- Encourage students to come up with unique ways to publish their writing. They might create classroom newsletters, charts, and illustrated comic books, as well as traditional reports and articles.

The Writing Process

1. Pre-Writing

- Decide what you want to write about.
- Brainstorm ideas about the topic.
- List places where you can find out more about the topic.
- Do your research.

2. Drafting

- Use the information from your research to write about the topic.
- Use your own words.
- Continue writing even if your sentences and paragraphs aren't perfect.
- Read your work to see if what you wrote is clear.
- Share it with others and listen to suggestions.

3. Revising

- Reread what you have written.
- Consider the suggestions that others make.
- Decide how you can make your writing better.
- Make your changes.
- Read your work aloud.

4. Proofreading

- Make sure all of your sentences are complete.
- Check for spelling, punctuation, and capitalization mistakes.
- Change words that are used incorrectly.
- Ask someone else to check your work.

5. Publishing

- Copy the corrected draft so there are no mistakes.
- Use your best penmanship.
- Share your writing with others.

CHAPTER 5

Physical Education, Art, and Music

Let's Get Physical: Fishbone Map

Skills Objective

Identify specific exercises appropriate for different body parts.

A **Fishbone Map** is a graphic organizer that gives students the opportunity to investigate multiple characteristics of a topic and then break down those characteristics into more specific details. In this activity, students create a fishbone map to identify various exercises that can strengthen and tone different parts of the body.

1. Start the activity by surveying students to determine what they already know about exercising. Ask questions such as: *What muscle groups are exercised by doing squats? If you want to strengthen your arms, what would be a good exercise to do?*

2. After your discussion, draw a fishbone map on the board and give students a copy of the **Let's Get Physical reproducible (page 91)**. Write

the topic, *Exercises for Different Body Parts,* in the center of the fishbone map, and direct students to do the same.

3. Point out how there are four "ribs" extending out from the main topic area. Explain that each rib represents an idea related to the main topic. In this case, each rib represents a different part of the body. Model writing the word *Arms* on one rib. Direct students to do the same. Invite students to choose other body parts for the remaining three ribs.

4. Point out how each rib has three lines attached to it. These lines are for recording details that go along with each main topic. Point to the rib where you wrote *Arms*. Explain that in this section of the map, you will record exercises designed for the arms. Ask students for suggestions of arm exercises and write three of them on the map. For example: *bicep curls, push-ups, overhead stretches.*

5. Tell students they will complete the map on their own. Make sure they understand how to record their ideas on the fishbone map before they begin working independently. Have students list names of exercises that are appropriate for the body parts that they listed.

6. Close the activity by having students demonstrate some of the exercises they listed on their maps.

Extended Learning

- Have students record the amount of time they exercise each day in an exercise log.

- Encourage students to make posters to show how different exercises are done. Invite them to demonstrate for the class.

- Have students design a simple exercise routine that incorporates three different exercises for one body part.

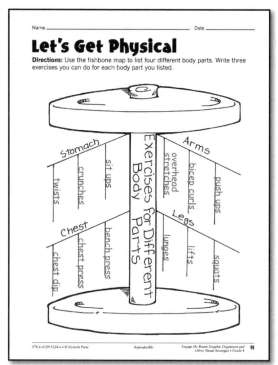

Let's Get Physical

Directions: Use the fishbone map to list four different body parts. Write three exercises you can do for each body part you listed.

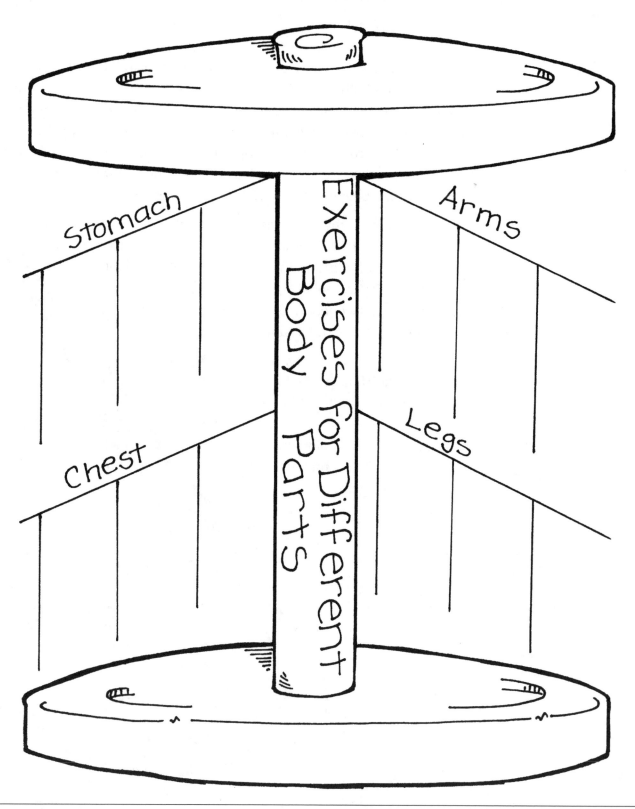

Color My World: Color Wheel

Materials

Color My World reproducible

large box of assorted crayons

colored chalk

paint palettes

paintbrushes

red, yellow, and blue paint

Skills Objectives

Understand the difference between primary, secondary, and tertiary colors.

Identify complementary and analogous colors on a color wheel.

A **Color Wheel** is a graphic organizer that shows the relationships between various colors. Most color wheels feature 12 colors. Primary colors (red, yellow, and blue) cannot be mixed or formed by any combination of other colors. Primary colors are the basis for all other colors. Secondary colors (green, orange, and purple) result from two primary colors being mixed together. For example, yellow and blue make green. Tertiary colors are made by combining a primary color, such as red, with a secondary color, such as orange. The result is red-orange. In this activity, students mix paints to create their own color wheels.

1. Begin this activity by passing a box of crayons around and asking each student to select one color. Ask students to tell you what colors they think were mixed together to create that color. Write the vocabulary words *primary, secondary,* and *tertiary* on the board and define them for students.

2. Give students a copy of the **Color My World reproducible (page 94)**. Explain that they will use paint to fill in the color wheel. Tell students that a color wheel places colors in order based on how they are mixed together.

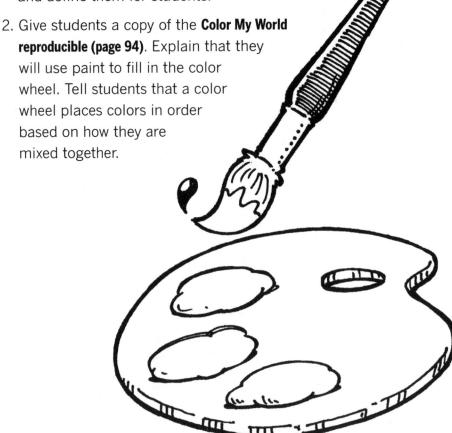

3. Draw a sample color wheel on the board, and use colored chalk to fill in the sections for primary colors. Give each student a paint palette with the primary colors and a paintbrush. Direct students to paint the primary colors on their color wheels.

4. Point out that the spaces for the secondary colors fall between the primary colors. To paint a secondary color, you mix together the two primary colors on either side of it. Demonstrate how to mix blue and yellow to make the color green.

5. Make sure students understand how to determine which colors are mixed to create secondary colors before directing them to work independently to fill in the spaces for purple and orange. Invite students to use their paint to fill in the spaces for the tertiary colors as well.

6. When color wheels are completed, write the words *complementary* and *analogous* on the board. Tell students that complementary colors are directly opposite from each other on the color wheel. Analogous colors are any three colors which are side by side on the color wheel. Explain that artists use complementary colors and analogous colors in their paintings to create different moods and to balance their work.

7. Close the activity by having students paint a picture using their color wheels as a guide for selecting colors. Encourage students to use either complementary colors or analogous colors in their paintings.

Extended Learning

- Have students experiment with tints and shades of color. Encourage them to mix two primary colors together and then add bits of white to make various tints of the color and bits of black to make various shades.

- Ask students to title and display their artwork. Encourage them to compare and contrast the different pieces and identify various "levels" of color.

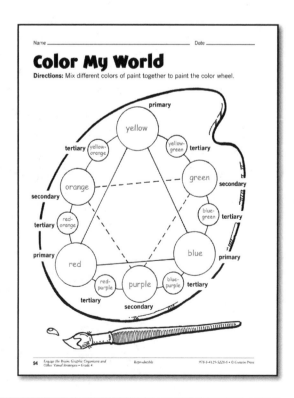

Name _____ Date _____

Color My World

Directions: Mix different colors of paint together to paint the color wheel.

primary

yellow

tertiary (yellow-orange)

yellow-green) tertiary

green

secondary

orange

secondary

blue-green) tertiary

tertiary (red-orange)

primary

blue

primary

red

red-purple

purple

blue-purple) tertiary

tertiary

secondary

Color My World

Directions: Mix different colors of paint together to paint the color wheel.

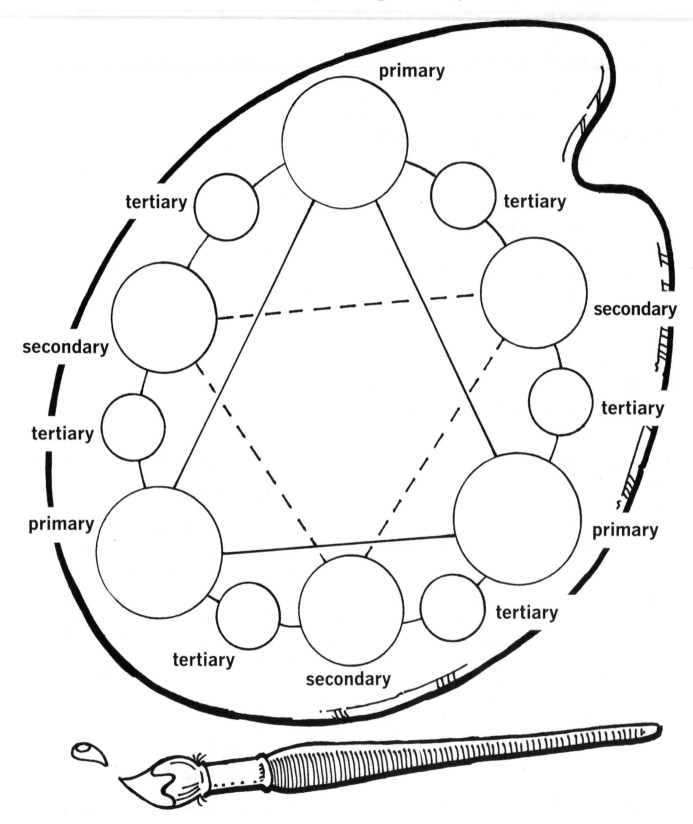

Engage the Brain: Graphic Organizers and Other Visual Strategies • Grade 4   *Reproducible*   978-1-4129-5228-6 • © Corwin Press